"Stop publication of this book! These tips are supposed to be secret!"
— John Badham, director of *Saturday Night Fever, War Games, Blue Thunder*

"Mark Travis's new book, *The Film Director's Bag of Tricks*, could only be written by a director of vast experience and practical knowledge that, thankfully, he's willing to share with the rest of us. Both of his books, and his class, should be compulsory in every film school in America."
— Cyrus Nowrasteh, director of *The Stoning of Soraya M.*

"This book is smart, incisive, and a valuable, lively read. Mark gets it and sends it on to the reader with energy and wit."
— Arthur Seidelman, director of television and theater

"Mark Travis knows a thing or two about directing. Having worked with him at Yale and again last year, I have seen the magic of his 'bag of tricks' up close. He's amazing. Enjoy the read."
— Henry Winkler, actor, director, producer

"A really good book for directors and actors. It is entertaining, instructive, and not too long. What more do you want?"
— Gordon Hunt, director, casting director

"Mark Travis has taken the mysterious job of the director and translated it into specific techniques that actually work. This is a must-read for the serious director."
— John Truby, script consultant, teacher

"A must-have for aspiring and novice directors, actors, and writers. Travis' experience and expertise as an actor, director, and writer will provide filmmakers with a dizzying array of techniques that will produce dazzling scenes, authentic performances, and memorable moments on film."
— Don Schwartz, writer for *CineSource* magazine

"Being a film director with one movie under my belt, I look forward to using the 'tricks' Mr. Travis writes about in his book on my next project. Whether you're a seasoned pro, or a novice like me, you won't go wrong with this book in your back pocket."
— Matthew Terry, filmmaker, screenwriter, teacher, columnist for hollywoodlitsales.com

"In *The Film Director's Bag of Tricks*, Mark Travis takes you into the eye of a director. With deep intention to empower the writer and the actor, he shows you all the tricks of the trade. His process unifies the visions of the director, writer and actor in a collaborative effort to bring the script to life. This creates an artistic expression that best brings out the voice of the story. He guides you through some exercises such as: the Socratic method, creating the 'safe zone,' Pause and Clip, Comfort and Conflict, Break the Continuum, and the power of Adding and Subtracting Characters. Through these methods and more, he awakens the possibility in all the players to transform the story into a work of art."

> — Jen Grisanti, story/career consultant, author of *Story Line: Finding Gold In Your Life Story*, writing instructor for NBC's Writers on the Verge

"Writers should read it, actors should read it, but most of all, directors have to read this one. These are ways to help directors, writers, and actors to communicate their needs better. It's not about tricking everyone to do what you want, but about finding the tools needed to make the film everyone will be proud of. The information here is told with a wonderful perspective, and to top it off, in the last chapter we get six interviews with other directors, each telling their own perspective on the art of directing."

> — Erin Corrado, OneMovieFiveReviews.com

"Mark disproves the old adage 'You can't teach an old dog new tricks.' I certainly learned a few."

> — Stu Berg, director

"Several years ago I was fortunate enough to attend a workshop given by Mark Travis. From the flood of ideas that evening I took away one simple 'trick' that has worked magic in my storytelling ever since. How thrilling to see that Mark has filled his latest book with similar techniques. His years of experience boiled down into a fun, effective and easy-to-execute bag of tricks? Fantastic!"

> — Jay Miles, author of *Conquering YouTube*

"*The Film Director's Bag of Tricks* is full of fresh ideas and concepts that open your mind. You will find many creative tricks to create a brilliant working relationship with the writer, director, and actors. This book is a useful tool and a major benefit for directors."

> — Carole Dean, author of *The Art of Film Funding*

"Mark Travis' new book *The Film Director's Bag of Tricks* is an invaluable tool for all directors, be you newcomer or seasoned pro. Having work with Mark for over ten years I have not only seen the tricks in action, but have had the opportunity to put many of them to use in my own work. The 'Bag of Tricks' can help you to achieve your desired results in a way that is both organic, subtle and sophisticated."
— Frederick Johntz, writer, director, producer

"Mark brings 'God's Little Workshop' to all of us. Writers. Directors. Actors. Thank God that he exists and keeps on writing these wonderful books. I still work with the techniques he taught me in every film I make. What a wonderful bag of tricks. Thanks Mark."
— Annette Ernst, director

"Your greatest shots and scenes are worth nothing if you don't know how to get the most out of your writers and actors. The ideas in this book are shortcuts to brilliance, giving everybody the space to be creative even when the clock is ticking. These are deceptively simple ways to calm, inspire and encourage people to move beyond their limits. It can take years of struggle to work out a handful of techniques, so it is a gift to have so many rich ideas in one book."
— Christopher Kenworthy, author of *Master Shots*, director of *The Sculptor*

"I pretty much owe my career to the guidance of director Mark W. Travis, so I'm happy to recommend his latest book for film directors. In it, he provides what he calls 'tricks' (but what are really just psychologically effective methods of persuasion) which will ease the process between a director and the writers and actors with whom he collaborates. In addition to the methods, there are wonderful interviews with major directors such as Mark Rydell, John Badham, and Jan Eliasberg discussing the usage of these methods. For directors (and for writers and actors as well), this is a remarkable and valuable tool."when the clock is ticking. These are deceptively simple ways to calm, inspire and encourage people to move beyond their limits. It can take years of struggle to work out a handful of techniques, so it is a gift to have so many rich ideas in one book."
— Jim Beaver, actor, writer

THE FILM DIRECTOR'S
Bag Of Tricks

How to get what you want from writers and actors

Mark W. Travis

Published by Michael Wiese Productions
12400 Ventura Blvd. #1111
Studio City, CA 91604
tel. 818.379.8799
fax 818.986.3408
mw@mwp.com
www.mwp.com

Cover design: Johnny Ink *www.johnnyink.com*
Book design: Gina Mansfield Design

Printed by McNaughton & Gunn, Inc., Saline, Michigan
Manufactured in the United States of America

Library of Congress Cataloging-in-Publication Data

Travis, Mark W., 1943–
 The film director's bag of tricks : how to get what you want
from writers and actors / Mark W. Travis.
     p. cm.
 ISBN 978-1-61593-056-2
 1. Motion pictures--Production and direction. I. Title.
 PN1995.9.P7T78 2011
 791.4302'3--dc22

                                                    2011017279

Dedication

It's the Fall of 2001 and I've been visiting Mom for several days. It's hard. It's difficult. It's a huge strain. Half of the time I don't know if she really knows that I'm there. Or even who I am. She enjoys me. She appreciates me. But she's not the same, not the same Mother I've known for the past fifty years. She's not the Mother that I've always known that I can rely on, count on, lean on. She's a memory of that Mother. A mere suggestion.

We're sitting on the couch at the foot of her bed. Looking through old photographs. Outside the room I can hear the other residents shuffling, talking, arguing. Conversations that are going unheeded, unnoticed. Conversations of the distant and the dying.

But I'm determined to connect, even if it is just for a moment.

"So, Mom, I'm really struggling. I don't know if what I am doing is going to work. I'm scared. I've failed so many times in my life. I've made so many bad decisions. And I'm afraid I might do it again, and again. And I miss our late night phones calls and you listening to me and giving me that comfort and guidance and love that somehow kept me going. And I don't know what I'm going to do without that."

I look into my Mother's eyes and I can see the twinkle, the sparkle that has been there for nearly ninety years. And I see the distant look that used to mean that she was deep in thought and that I needed to be patient and quiet — and perhaps on guard. But, now I'm not sure what it means. Now I'm not sure she will come back. I'm not sure she's heard me. I'm not sure she's there.

It's 1953. I'm ten years old and I have just finished reading the biography of George Washington Carver. I want to be like him. I want to dedicate my life to the discovery of the mysteries of the universe. Like George Washington Carver I want to give my laboratory the name "God's Little Workshop."

I'm in the basement. I'm making a sign. It's going to be perfect. I know I'm not as smart as George Washington Carver, but I do know that I can fix things — toasters, irons, record players — anything that's broken. Mom even told me I had a gift, that I'm talented. So I'm going to announce my own little workshop to the world — or at least to the town — or at least to the people going by on the street. And they can bring me their broken things and I'll fix them. It'll be perfect. "God's Little Workshop."

It's a half an hour later and the sign is now sitting out in the front of the house — waiting. It's waiting outside and I'm waiting inside. Waiting for someone to stop. Waiting for somebody who wants some help. I want to help somebody. But nobody's stopping. They all keep driving by or walking by. Maybe the sign isn't big enough. Maybe they don't understand that my little workshop is a place where....

"Mark, what's this?"

Mom is standing in front of me. She seems upset (maybe), or confused (maybe). I can't tell.

"Mark, is this your sign?"

"Yeah, Mom. Isn't it great? Just like George Washington Carver. You know, he called his workshop where he did all his experiments on peanuts and all the things you can do with peanuts — 'God's Little Workshop' — because he felt that it wasn't him that was so smart or brilliant but that it was really the work of God that was working inside him making him see things that maybe other people couldn't see and he knew he was doing something wonderful for the rest of the world and he wanted people to know that it was really God working through him."

"Mark…"

"And I want to be like him and do wonderful things and even though I know you think I'm talented and gifted — I don't really think so. I don't think so at all. I think maybe, like George Washington Carver, it's just God's work because I don't know how I know what I know or how I can do what I can do…."

"Mark!"

And there's that look. That faraway look that says that maybe I should be quiet. Maybe I've said too much. Maybe I've done the wrong thing — again. And so I go quiet — and I wait. And the faraway look drifts back to me and she's looking right at me with that twinkle and love and patience that can only be my Mom.

Then she says something she has said many, many times.

"My dear dope."

I know that if anyone else heard her say that to me they might think it wasn't nice. But I know what she means. There's more love in 'my dear dope' then there is in a hundred thousand kisses.

"My dear dope, you *are* talented. You *are* gifted. And you don't have to understand how you know what you know or how you can do what you do. It's your job to put these talents and gifts to good use. That's all. And it's your job to take credit for who you are. Be proud of yourself, Mark. Be proud of who you are and the gifts you have. Celebrate yourself. Let the world know that Mark Travis has something to offer. And one way to do that would be to call your workshop, 'Mark's Little Workshop.'"

And I sat there and looked at her, a bit confused and a bit hurt. I really thought 'God's Little Workshop' was a far better name. I mean, everyone knew who God was and I was sure that nobody knew who Mark was.

I never made the new sign that said "Mark's Little Workshop." I think I was convinced that it would never attract any attention. And I gave up the idea of having my own little workshop that would be of service to the world — or the town — or the neighborhood. And I went back to keeping my gifts and my talents private.

And now it's over forty years later and I'm looking into her eyes again. And there's the distant look again. But this time I know she's not coming back. She may have heard me. But she's too far away. It's too long a distance. And I know that in a moment she'll look at me and there'll be no 'dear dope.' There will only be a sad smile and a 'isn't it wonderful what they've done with this room.' And I drift into that lonely room where I go sometimes, knowing I've lost my Mom forever.

I pick up my suitcase, ready to head for the airport. I have only a few moments left with her on this trip — and who knows what she's going to be like — or who she's going to be when I see her next. She turns to me, coming back from that distant place. The twinkle is there. The glow is there. But where is she?

"Mark, listen to me."

Suddenly it's my Mom. My Mom's voice. My Mother. She's back. After all these years, she's back.

"Mark, my dear Mark. You know you have always made the right decisions. The fact that things don't turn out as planned is not your fault. Perhaps that was the way it was meant to be. You are who you were meant to be. You have to trust that. You have to trust yourself. And you have to trust that God does have a plan for you and it is only your job to do the best you can with the talents and gifts that He has given you. I believe in you, Mark. You just need to believe in yourself. And the late-night phone calls are not over. They happen every night because every night I go to sleep talking to every one of my children, and grandchildren, and Popi. Every night we talk. You and me. And I'm always here for you. I love you. You know that."

And then she looks away, at the furniture, at the walls, at the pictures of years of our family hanging on those walls. "Isn't it wonderful what they've done with this room."

Good night, Mom. Tonight we'll have another talk.

Dedicated to my mother: Harriet Small Travis

Table of Contents

Acknowledgments

Every time I sit down to write another book I am struck by the overwhelming realization that this is truly a collaborative effort. It is not the same collaboration as filmmaking because the writing of a book is a solitary process buoyed up and supported by a host of magnificent people who believe in you, trust in you, and want you to be your best.

The Film Director's Bag of Tricks could not have existed without the incredible support, belief and passion of the following:

First, my good friend and patient publisher, Michael Wiese, who first conceived of the idea (even came up with the title) and waited for several years while I got my act together. And to Ken Lee of Michael Wiese Productions for his avid support and for helping me to keep my eye on the ball.

It was always my intention to include the tools and techniques of other directors. I am so grateful for the time and honest revelations of the following directors who I am pleased and honored to call friends: Mark Rydell, Arthur Seidelman, John Badham, Gordon Hunt, Will Mackenzie, and Jan Eliasberg. Thank you, Jen Sagaio, for transcribing all those interviews and overseeing the formatting and proofreading.

When you write a book, it is really important to send out the unpublished manuscript to friends and colleagues, asking for critical notes and quotes. To those brave souls who ploughed through this book in rough form and gave me their honest feedback, I say "bless you, thank you" — Arthur

Seidelman, Jan Eliasberg, Henry Winkler, Mark Rydell, Cyrus Nowrasteh, John Truby, Asaad Kelada, John Badham, Gordon Hunt, Jeremy Kagan, Marty Pasetta, Fred Johntz, Martin Landau, Selise Eisman, Gil Bettman, Frank South, and of course my wife, Dianne Travis, for her encouragement and support.

And, finally, to all my students, colleagues, friends, and associates worldwide who have participated in the constant exploration, experimentation, discovery, and definition of these tricks: Bless you all — these tricks belong to you.

How To Use This Book

If you are a director, or just considering becoming a director, you will find this book enormously useful in many different ways. First, be clear on how the book is structured: Chapter One (Working with the Writer), Chapter Two (The Casting Process), Chapter Three (The Rehearsal Process) and Chapter Four (The Production Process). And then as a bonus we have Chapter Five, which contains in-depth interviews with six amazing directors. Don't feel like you have to read this book in order. Skip around. If you're about to go into rehearsal, read Chapter Three. If you're about to work with a writer, read Chapter One. Or if you are just curious about other directors and how they work, read Chapter Five.

And then check out the Table of Contents. You'll see all the tricks listed there. Pick a trick, read about it. And if you're really courageous and curious, invite some actor friends over and experiment. Read the trick out loud and then try it and see what happens.

For beginning directors I suggest that you settle in and read the book straight through. Each chapter, each trick, and each page will be a revelation to you and you will gain a deeper insight into the complex world of directing. Then move on and experiment.

For veteran directors I would suggest that you skim quickly through the Table of Contents and find those tricks that will immediately address the challenges you have faced with writers and actors. Pick through the book and you will find solutions to problems you have dealt with in the past and you will find descriptions of tricks that you have already been using that will give you new insights into your skills.

For actors I highly recommend that you read every page of Chapters Two, Three, and Four. There is nothing like having the covers pulled off those techniques that directors use on you. And, besides learning these tricks, you will also begin to see yourself, how resistant you are, how stubborn or uncertain, and why these tricks are so important and so valuable. And you will most likely begin to recognize within yourself the tricks that you use in order to get what you want from a director. Remember, this works both ways.

And for writers, of course you must read Chapter One. It's all about you. John Badham was right when he said, "These tips were supposed to be kept secret." But now that they are exposed you will understand more clearly the complex psychological relationship between the writer and the director. Then read the remaining chapters. In the process of working with actors you will begin to understand more clearly what directors go through in order to stimulate the performances we need to make your written material come to life.

At the end of each chapter I have included Exercises (or homework) that will increase your experience of this book and help you learn how to incorporate these tools, tricks and techniques into your own directing. I suggest that you do these exercises with a partner (other than the hired actors). The more you engage in a dialogue with other writers, directors and actors as you are experimenting with these techniques, the more these tools will become an integral part of your process.

Finally, think of this book as a great guide, a menu of tricks, a toolbox that you can dip into at any time. Be willing to experiment, be willing to fail and try again. Be willing to explore this new world of directing tricks just as you would explore new restaurants, new clubs, new music, or new friends.

Foreword

I had the privilege of meeting Mark Travis some years back, and was so impressed by his knowledge of the craft of directing and his ability to articulate that knowledge in an insightful and accessible way that I hired him to be my assistant on the spot.

He had demonstrated his ability to communicate his insights with clarity and sensitivity. His ability to analyze dramatic material is formidable. In addition, he is able to communicate his insights with uncommon clarity and sensitivity.

He is able to deliver his thoughts in a constructive and un-threatening manner. This skill is essential for a teacher, and even more so for a director. I have great faith in him and very high expectations for his future.

This book reveals with articulate clarity his skills at communication. In most cases I am disappointed when artists try to analyze their craft. I don't feel that way about Mark's writing. He comfortably demonstrates his intelligence and comprehensive insights into the craft of directing. He has done so with keen perception and passion. I compliment him for achieving clarity and insight in discussing the director's task.

Mark Rydell, director, producer
Los Angeles, 2010

Introduction

Many of you have read one of my other books, either *The Director's Journey* or *Directing Feature Films*, and you are probably wondering what I am doing writing a book with the whimsical title *The Film Director's Bag of Tricks*.

Or you haven't read any of my books and you just picked this one up because you are one of those directors who doesn't want to have to read long chapters on theories and executions and would rather have shortcuts and quick guaranteed results. Don't worry, I understand, I'm just like you. Truthfully, I think I gravitated to directing theatre (and eventually television and film) because it looked easy or I thought I could fake it. And for years I did. I mixed pure instinct and intuition with an uncanny ability to justify my choices and actions with something sounding like educated reasoning. It worked like a charm until I was finally tested during those years at Yale (where for some reason they thought we really should study and learn and apply ourselves and get beyond instinct and intuition and make rational and reasonable choices). To please the powers that be at Yale, I did the work. But quite honestly it wasn't until many years later that I appreciated what they had put me through. Now I see it all coming together. Now I see that my instincts and intuitions are based in some morass of experience and education, whether I like it or not.

Once I realized this, I thought it would be much more interesting to really test myself, really challenge myself and see if I could find the zone where everything would fall apart — where instinct and intuition would do nothing but lead me astray. But no matter how much I pushed and probed, I couldn't find that place. Somehow my outrageous ideas and impractical approaches kept working. They kept producing amazing results. Well, as you can imagine, this was very frustrating. Not that I don't like magical results. I do. But what was displeasing me was that I couldn't prove to myself that I was the fraud I always believed I was. Somewhere in my creative world, that indefinable nether region where magical muses romp and play, there was a logical and rational force guiding the chaos. I'd push harder and the forces would keep finding the logic. Then eventually I gave up the game. I surrendered and just decided to allow myself to play. I decided to stop questioning, stop reasoning, and especially to stop trying to make sense of it all.

In a scene from one of my favorite films, *Shakespeare In Love*, written by Marc Norman and Tom Stoppard and directed by John Madden, a theatre manager, Philip Henslowe (Geoffrey Rush), is being threatened by a financier, Hugh Fennyman (Tom Wilkinson):

                    HENSLOWE
        What have I done, Mr. Fennyman?

                    FENNYMAN
        The theatres are all closed by the
        Plague!

                    HENSLOWE
        Oh, that.

                    FENNYMAN
        By order of the Master of the Revels!

```
                    HENSLOWE
          Mr. Fennyman, let me explain about
          the theatre business.

(they stop)

          The natural condition is one of
          insurmountable obstacles on the
          road to imminent disaster. Believe
          me, to be closed by the plague is
          a bagatelle in the ups and downs
          of owning a theatre.

                    FENNYMAN
          So what do we do?

                    HENSLOWE
          Nothing. Strangely enough, it all
          turns out well.

                    FENNYMAN
          How?

                    HENSLOWE
          I don't know. It's a mystery.
```

"I don't know. It's a mystery." That's how I feel about directing. It is truly mysterious. I have no idea how or why it works. Oh yes, I know, I have written two other books about directing where I explain in great detail how it works. And I have been praised by some of the finest directors in Hollywood for "taking the mystery out of directing" or for "making clear what we have all understood only by instinct." Fine, so I have the ability to bring clarity to a process that is as vague and confusing as the Bush Administration's foreign policy. And I am glad that this clarity is helpful to so many. But, honestly, way down deep inside I do know that all of us, all directors, are simply practicing sleight-of-hand. Not only do we create an illusion of reality (on the screen or on the stage), but we are also very adept at creating the illusion that we know what the hell we are doing. Not a bad job if you can get it.

About a year ago I was teaching one of my directing work-shops in Cornwall, England. I was fortunate enough to have been invited by the Media Centre Cornwall to help initiate a new program intended to stimulate and support the filmmakers of Cornwall. And I was doubly honored to have Michael Wiese, my publisher, attend the workshop. As I was trying to cram what should have been hours and hours of teaching into a few days, I found myself wanting to take shortcuts. "Cut to the chase," said a little voice in my head. Now, being one of those persons who listens to the voices in his head (and often has heated debates with them… more on this later), I found myself saying: "Let me show you a trick." And I would demonstrate a shortcut, a technique, a 'trick' if you will, that would produce the desired result almost instantaneously. This is when the muses are really having a good time. They are at their most mischievous. They know they are going to dazzle. They know it is all artifice and trickery and that it creates the illusion of reality. The muses are wicked and wonderful, devious and delightful, not to be trusted and not to be ignored. Thank God we have them.

And after I had demonstrated five or six tricks, Michael turned to me with that twinkle he gets when he knows he has a brilliant idea. "I know what your next book should be," he said. I looked at him with both dread and delight. Delighted that he had an idea for a new book. Dread that I would have to plunge myself once again into that painful process called writing. "The Film Director's Bag of Tricks." Well, once again he was right. And once again I stalled for as long as I could.

There are a lot of reasons for this book and quite likely none of them are any good, but they will have to suffice. The reality is that for over a dozen years I have been teaching directing all over the world. And it is true that through my style and approach to teaching this elusive craft I have saved directors years of exploration and trial and error by just demonstrating what I lovingly call a 'trick.' Truth is that I don't know what else to call these short cuts. You could call them tools or techniques and that makes it all sound much more legitimate, but in reality they are tricks. They are sleight-of-hand. And most often the writer, the actor, and even the audience is seduced into thinking that something quite different has occurred.

All directing is sleight-of-hand. Think about it. Whether it is stage or film, all we are doing is telling a simple story. Perhaps it is a complex story, but regardless, it is a story with a beginning, middle, and end. We are telling this story in a compressed time frame (usually about two hours) because of the attention span of our audience. Novelists don't have this restriction. They can write long and detailed stories because the time commitment for the reader is flexible. But in theatre, film, and television, we have a window of time with the audience. So we compress our story, we create a 'script' that will guide us through. We rehearse, shoot and edit using sleight-of-hand in order to make the audience feel or believe that something real is actually happening. And like the audience at a magic show, our audience wants to believe. They want to believe in the magic. They don't want the magician to explain how it is done. Yes, I know, deep down inside we all want to know, but once we are told, once the curtain is lifted, we will immediately resent the magician because he has destroyed the illusion.

Let's face the facts. We are in a business of illusion. We create and tell stories that are not real, not true. They may be based on a true story, but what is happening on the screen

xxvi THE FILM DIRECTOR'S BAG OF TRICKS ~ Mark W. Travis

is not true. Even the most determined documentaries are a reworking of what may have been true at one time. So we are in the business of selling myths and imaginings. We rest on the audience's suspension of disbelief. We manipulate the audience and we pull a veil over their eyes and ask them to believe.

And as directors we are always using sleight-of-hand to get writers and actors to deliver what we need so that we can create our next illusion. That's what this book is about: The tricks we use with writers and actors in the process of creating an illusion.

If you have read one of my other books, you may have noticed that this book has a totally different tone. It's lighter, a bit more irreverent. That's because we are looking at the directing process through an entirely different lens. We're going to pull back the curtain and expose an aspect of directing that many directors use but may never admit. It's not just that we create illusions, it is that we, as directors, are willing to do almost anything to get what we want, to get the job done. We may not be proud of these techniques, but we know that they work. We know that when the clock is ticking, the sun is going down, or the actress is about to quit, we have to pull a rabbit out of the hat and get the job done.

Basically, no matter how you look at it, we directors are alchemists. My favorite definition of alchemy: *Any magical power or process of transmuting a common substance, usually of little value, into a substance of great value.* Perfect. That's what directors do. We take that common substance that is of little value and make it into something of perceived great value through some magical process.

Let's get started.

The Alchemist and The Story and The Writer

There is only one place to start the journey —
with the story or the idea, the first substance of
little value. And I say that it has 'little value' because truthfully it is just an idea, an inkling, an
urging at the edge of consciousness. It tickles us
and provokes us, but by itself it has little value.
Yet it is one of the most essential elements in
our alchemic experiment. It's the one we have
to begin with, because without it we will create
a truly useless brew.

And usually attached to this story or idea is a
thing called the writer — a necessary but often
troublesome element in our process. It is with
this writer that we have to begin working our
sleight-of-hand, our magic, our little tricks that
will produce the results that we need.

Note: We could stop here and begin to discuss
how writing itself is highly accomplished magic,
sleight-of-hand, illusion upon illusion. But this is
a book about directing and I will deal with the
complex nature of writing and storytelling in my
next book.

In no particular order, here are some goodies from the Director's Bag of Tricks to be used with the writer.

TRICK: EXPRESSING ENTHUSIASM

In his brilliant book, *On Directing*, Harold Clurman said: "First, express enthusiasm." Words of wisdom. Many writers are pesky, problematic, paranoid, and totally convinced that their work is genius. God love 'em. They are brilliant and talented and have the constitutions of an adolescent. I know this to be true because I am quite clearly one of them. So, the trick: "First express enthusiasm."

A specific aspect of this trick is that the enthusiasm has to be genuine. It has to be honest. You can't say that you love the script, the story, the scene or the character when you really don't. Not only are most writers really good at creating credible characters, they are also very good at sniffing out insincerity. They can see it and smell it before you've even finished spinning it. So you have to be honest *and* you have to express enthusiasm. If you truly hate everything about the script, then you really shouldn't be having this discussion. So there must be something in the script or the story that you genuinely love. Even if it is only the potential. Find it. Hold on to it. Praise it. Now you will have the writer in your hand.

Example:

Several years ago I was being considered to direct a project. I read it (had to read it overnight for a meeting the next day with the producers) and I was disappointed with the script. It was well-intentioned, but confusing. In the center of the story, however, there was one scene that was truly magical, a love scene. Thinking about it on my way to the meeting it occurred to me that we would have a very strong project if the rest of the script had been conceived and written as well as that love scene. I had been told the writer was one of the producers (interviewing me) so I knew I had to be very careful. Of course, one of the first questions they asked me was, "How did you like the script?" Now, I know the drill. You don't get the job by saying you don't like the script, especially when the writer is one of the producers and the other producer is his wife! So, "express enthusiasm" is in order.

"So, Mark, how do you like the script?"

"Amazing! Great story!"

Please understand that I said 'great story,' not 'great script.' And it was, truly, a great story. It's just the script that was inadequate. That was very clear to me.

"Great story! You know, there is something about the love scene and how that is conceived and shaped that gave me insight into how the rest of the story can work."

Again, reference to story and not script. Now the writer is looking at me, and I look straight into his eyes — time for sleight-of-hand.

"When I read that scene I realized what you were writing. The magical energy of that scene is really the clue and the guide to the entire film. It made me realize that we are in a world that is full of electricity and that this energy can be harnessed to either serve us or destroy us."

At this moment the writer is beaming. Maybe I laid it on too thick, I'm not sure. But I have to keep going, they are all listening.

"Look, this is a fantastic story full of pain and promise, deceit and dedication (all true), and I would be thrilled to be a part of the team that would bring it to the screen."

The writer is now beside himself. I think I can stop. I look to his wife and she is smiling. Then he says:

> "You are the first person who has truly seen my script for what it really is."

Interesting — I never mentioned the script, only one scene. The sleight-of-hand has worked. The other producers are also thrilled. The rest of the interview goes very well and we even get into initial discussions of some rewrites to bring the 'magic of the love scene' to the rest of the material.

I leave feeling good, but with a bit of concern, because I am aware of the amount of work that will need to be done.

Ironic ending: I get a call two days later that goes something like this:

> "Good news. We loved your interview and your insights into the script and the story. We want you to direct this film. But... (and you could feel the other very large and heavy shoe hovering from the 'good news' at the beginning)... we have just lost our funding. The wife of the financier read the script and didn't like it."

Well, so much for my sleight-of-hand. I got the job, but the wife of the financier was much more blunt and killed the project. To this date this film has not been made.

TRICK: THE HIDDEN STORY

Seeing something wonderful in the script that is not really there.

This is a biggie. You read a script and you see what *is* there. But are you able to look beyond that and see what the story *could* be? This is your job. As the director you must see not just what is obvious and on the page, you must see what is possible.

Note: There are no tricks for doing this. There is no sleight-of-hand that will suddenly allow your imagination and insight to flourish. You come by this through experience, imagination, courage, magical muses, and the courage to dig into your own life experience.

So now let's assume that you can see, feel, hear and imagine a world of events and situations that are not contained in the script at all, but are stimulated by what is on the page. What do you do? You can't go to the writer and say, "Hey, great script, but I've got a much better idea." That won't fly. You know that you are not interested in the script as is, but you are truly intrigued with what it could be.

Now, here's the trick. Your job is to get the writer to do one of two things (or both). First, lead the writer to visualize or imagine the elements that you see in your head. But you want the writer to think that he/she came up with them. Second, get the writer to believe that the elements you imagine in your head are actually in the script.

The Story
Here's the hypothetical story. John and Carol are a married couple. Their marriage is in jeopardy, on the rocks. Carol is spending a lot of time with her male friend, Allen, but it's not an affair, not infidelity. They are just very good and close friends. What is challenging the marriage is boredom. And you (the reader/director) keep thinking it has to be more than boredom. Either there is an affair, or fear of an affair, or the desire for an affair — by either Carol or John. Trust and fidelity have to be threatened in order to make this story truly interesting.

First step
Express enthusiasm. Something like this:

> "This is great. A relationship that is threatened by ennui, boredom, complacency. Very delicate and potentially very powerful."

Second step

Once you have expressed honest enthusiasm you say something like:

> "You know that moment when John intimates to Carol that he knows she was having an affair?"

And the writer will tell you that there is no such moment in the script.

> "What, that's not in there? Wow, I could have sworn it was."

And again she will affirm that it is not there.

> "Amazing. This is what I love about your script, the subtextual life is so powerful I can feel events happening that are just below the surface."

This may just bring silence — a silence of appreciation or uncertainty.

> "But he does believe that she is, doesn't he?"

All you are trying to do is add this element to the relationship. Implying that the script, on its own, is suggesting this to you (which is saying that others who read it will also get the same implication) will be almost impossible for the writer to ignore. The writer will have to take this into consideration. The important thing here: The writer will *not* feel like this was a suggestion from you, but rather that there is an element in the script lurking in the subtext that has to be considered and either strengthened (which will fulfill your goal) or eliminated. I defy any writer to eliminate something from a script that never existed in the first place.

Socratic Questioning

Leading the writer to discover something that is not there, but that you want to be there, is tricky. Socratic Questioning is a tool that is the key to this process. Use questions — not statements or suggestions — just questions.

> **Note:** This process will be used extensively throughout this book, so there is one basic dynamic you must be aware of. When you ask someone a question (even though you may be implying a specific answer), the answer comes from the other person, not from you. And that is precisely what you want. You want the writer (and in future chapters, the actor) to discover and articulate what you already know or believe. If, on the other hand, this new idea is simply stated by you to the writer, then it comes from you and it will always feel imposed from outside, inserted. At the core of the creative process of the writer (and actor) are impulse, intuition and instinct. And this source for material and ideas is more trusted and respected than anything from outside. Our goal is to stimulate that core with simple and innocent questions, knowing that regardless of the response we can lead the writer (actor) to 'discover' what we already know or believe.

This is all based on the Socratic method, also known as Socratic Questioning. For more information on Socratic Questioning, go to: *http://serc.carleton.edu/introgeo/socratic/second.html.*

Although Socratic Questioning appears simple, it is, in fact, intensely rigorous. As described in the writings of Plato, a student of Socrates, the teacher (director) feigns ignorance about a given subject in order to acquire another person's (writer or actor) fullest possible knowledge of the topic. Individuals have the capacity to recognize contradictions, so

Socrates assumed that incomplete or inaccurate ideas would be corrected during the process of disciplined questioning, and hence would lead to progressively greater truth and accuracy.

Okay, back to our discussion with the writer. It could go something like this:

> "Carol is having an affair with Allen, right?"
> "No."

> "Of course not. But she spends a lot of time with him."
> "Right."

> "And John is jealous of this time spent with Allen?"
> "Yes."

> "And doesn't he feel slightly abandoned?"
> "Yeah, sure."

> "But he doesn't think she's having an affair?"
> "No. He knows she's not."

> "How?"
> "He trusts her."

> "I see. Yet he feels abandoned and that doesn't feel good. Does he tell her that he feels abandoned?"
> "No. He trusts her."

> "I see. So he keeps these feelings of abandonment hidden and secret. Why?"
> "He doesn't want to upset her."

> "With telling her the truth?"
> "Well, it would upset her...."

> "...if he told her the truth. That he's feeling abandoned. And probably jealous and envious. And he's probably afraid that she will think that he is thinking that she's having an affair. Even though that is not what he is thinking."

And then silence. Let that all just hang. If the writer doesn't bite, you can follow up with:

"Does Carol want to have an affair?"
"No, she loves her husband too much."

"Too much to have an affair or too much to think about having an affair?"
"She's not going to have an affair."

"Good. So she's never thought about it."
(the writer goes silent)

"And John? Has he thought about it?"
"I don't think either of them ever think about having affairs. This isn't a story about a couple who want to be romantically involved with other people. This is not a story about cheating or infidelity. It's a story about boredom."

"Which is why Carol spends so much time with Allen, right?"
"Yes."

"Because she is bored with John."
"Yes."

"And John is feeling abandoned and perhaps envious or jealous?"
"Right."

"And Carol is getting some of her needs fulfilled in her relationship with Allen… needs that maybe John used to fulfill but for some reason doesn't anymore. Is that right?"
"Exactly. But they are not having an affair."

"What is your definition of an affair?"

And silence again. These silences are important. Writers, like actors, need time to process new ideas, insights or possibilities.

It may even take a day or two, but quite possibly this writer will come back with:

> "John thinks it could be an affair only because it feels like one. And even though he totally trusts her, he doesn't want her to know what he is thinking, because that would upset her. So he tells her nothing. And he pulls a little further away and the 'cloud of boredom' becomes darker."

And in your head you say 'Bingo!'

Pulling Back the Curtain

Now you are getting an idea how these tricks work. They are truly sleight-of-hand. They are manipulative, playful, and a bit devious... but honest. They work, and in my experience, even when the sleight-of-hand is revealed to the unsuspecting recipient (writer, actor, or audience), they respond with wonder and delight. And much like children at a magic show, they want you to do it again. You would think that they would be offended, annoyed, resentful, or even downright angry. The truth is that we all want to be seduced into doing what we are capable of doing or seeing what we want to see. We really don't want the curtain pulled back so we can see the wizard at the controls. And even when the curtain is pulled, we smile sadly, hoping that it will drop back into place and the magic will continue.

TRICK: THE HIDDEN SUBTEXT

Seeing subtext in order to stimulate the text.

This is a slight variation on the last trick, "The Hidden Story."

We all know that film scripts are terribly sparse and really don't reveal the inner life of characters in the way a novel can. All we get is a description of the visuals, the behavior of the characters, and what the characters say. This is the great challenge of writing a screenplay and reading a screenplay. Truth is, the real life of the screenplay exists only in our imagination as we read. We project into the characters the feelings and thoughts and emotions that we imagine must be going on. Otherwise, why would they be saying and doing what they are saying and doing? Truthfully, there is nothing on the page except visuals, dialogue, and behavior, and the rest is all projection. Yes, I know, there are those writers who will do their best to open the doors to the internal worlds of the characters with their parentheticals or clever descriptions of the emotional or cerebral process of the characters. Yet, regardless of the skill of the writer to define the emotional landscape of the characters, we are all relying heavily on the reader's projection. And this reality, this reliance, is just another opportunity for sleight-of-hand.

When I read a scene and report that I can feel the pain and anguish of shame in the woman, who is to say I am wrong? It's my projection, my experience, and I am welcome to it. If I tell the writer that I can feel the fear in a character as he boldly pronounces his new plans to his boss, who is to say this is not there? And let's say it's not there. Not at all. But I want it there. I think it needs to be there. And, most likely, it is clear that the writer never intended it or thought of it. But as a storyteller (and we are all storytellers, writers, directors and actors) I genuinely feel that this emotional state is a necessary and desirable aspect of the character. Now, I could simply make the suggestion to the writer.

> "Please add fear to this character. I think he is afraid of his own ideas, his own power, his own potential."

I could say that and now the writer is in a position of having to consider adjusting the character to fulfill my requests or desires. Or (and here is the sleight-of-hand), I could simply let the writer know that it is already there.

"I can feel it. Seems so clear to me every time I read it. It's wonderful."

I know I'm planting an idea in the writer's head, but (and here is the important part) I am giving him credit for it. It's not coming from me as a new idea. It is coming from his writing and from his characters. It's a compliment, not a criticism or complaint. And I also know that the writer is now going to view this 'insight' in a whole new way. He's going to consider whether or not he wants to kill something that seems to be peeking through one of his characters (something that he had not consciously intended), or if he wants to nurture and protect or even exploit this new facet of his character. The important thing here is that the writer is not thinking about me (the one who planted the idea). He's not thinking:

"Oh, the director wants me to change the character to be more like a character that he wants, for some reason."

No, he is most likely thinking,

"Hmm, I didn't think I was writing about that. I wonder where that came from. Interesting. Have to consider how this will affect the character and what I am trying to say."

And that is exactly where I want the writer to be. The magic is working. Then I just sit back and wait and watch and see how this writer is now incorporating or dealing with this new information. A writer wrestling with a new idea that seemed to come from deep within him will bring you his truth. A writer wrestling with a new idea that was thrust or imposed upon him from some outside source (you) will very likely bring you superficial or clichéd writing.

The Larger Picture
Seeing the picture you want to see but don't see — yet.

The trick above, "Hidden Subtext," has to do with a moment, with an aspect of the character, with a detail in the psychological make-up. But what if you are imagining something more global, more pervasive? We're getting back to that First Basic Step. Remember the "Nine Basic Steps Of Film Directing" in *Directing Feature Films*?

> **Note:** For those of you who haven't read my first two books, it's time for you to order *Directing Feature Films* from *amazon.com* or *mwp.com*. Turn to page 183. And for those of you who simply need to be reminded, here is the First Step.

> 1. *What is the story really all about?* What is the writer writing about? What is the subtextual theme or message that is coming through? What do you, as the director, want to say through the telling of this story?

Many times we read scripts and think, "This would be really great if it were about something more (profound, meaningful, funny, moving, political, social, insightful, playful... pick one)." And very likely you are right. At least you are right for you, for your tastes and desires and intentions. Maybe you feel the story would be stronger if you shifted genres (now there's a massive shift for the writer). But, how do you convince the writer of this change in direction, focus or genre? How do you pull the writer off the track she is going on and get her on your track without totally derailing the whole process? Time for another sleight-of-hand.

TRICK: REFRAMING THE PICTURE

Don't tell the writer what you want to see in the story. Tell her what you *do* see in the story (which is what you want to see) and give her all the credit for it.

Let's say it is a script about a young couple, strangers, who take a cross-country journey. Both want to get from the

East Coast to the West Coast for their own individual reasons. And they are driving the car belonging to a third party who simply wants his car delivered to the West Coast. It's a comedy. It's a road picture. It's the story of two strangers who form a deeper and more profound relationship through the experiences of this cross-country journey. You read it. You like the setup and the circumstances, but you are not interested in this little romantic comedy. You're looking for action-adventure, maybe even a thriller. And although this script is way off your radar screen, there is something in it that is holding you. And now you figure it out... it's the car! Why is this third character having his car driven cross-country? And suddenly you start to feel that there is a deeper and perhaps darker side to this story that resonates within you. A road comedy with a darkness lurking at every turn. Now you are truly excited about this project, but you are pretty sure that the writer had absolutely no intention of going down this darker path, and that just to suggest the idea might be disastrous. So, what to do? Here's the trick, the sleight-of-hand.

This new idea is *not* your idea. It is simply something that you 'discovered' in the text. Alright, I know it is your idea and you know it is your idea. But you can't let the writer know that. Well, you could but you know that might not work.

Remember, the script is only the written text; there is no written subtext. The subtext lurks beneath the text (unseen, unwritten but not unfelt). So, what you are feeling is this lurking darkness, this other storyline that has to do with the man and the car. And how you tell the writer about this subtextual urge goes something like this:

> "You know, I love this script (enthusiasm right up front, very important). It is funny, surprising, great characters, great love story, everything (even more

enthusiasm; it doesn't hurt as long as it is honest). And you know, as I was reading I was feeling this amazing energy rumbling underneath. This sort of mysterious tone, and I couldn't figure out where it was coming from or what you had done (important to give the writer credit) to create this. And then, on the second or third reading it struck me. It's the car and the mysterious and never-seen owner of the car. This is really a three-character story, not a two-character story. The car represents the third character, the man who wants his car driven cross-country, for some reason. And this creates mystery, intrigue, and a sense of impending danger."

Now you have laid the groundwork for a whole new tone for this film. The writer will very likely want to reject this idea because it was not her original intention. But it will be hard for her to totally reject it simply because you gave her credit for it. Just let her think about it. Don't press for agreement. It may take a while for this idea to get under her skin, but the first injection was painless and now all you need to do is wait for the medicine to take effect.

Subtext: The Sorcerer's Apprentice

By now you must be getting the idea that this sleight-of-hand depends heavily on the subtext. And you are right. Way to go! You are learning fast. And you will see during the rest of the book how we can use various forms and sources of subtext (with writers, actors, and even the audience) to persuade them to see what we see, feel what we feel, and believe what we believe.

TRICK: READING THE SCENE OUT LOUD

Reading the scene out loud is one of the most powerful tools you have. And it is a tool that must be used, because what we hear in our heads when we read a scene bears little resemblance to what will most likely happen when skilled actors embrace the material.

In *Directing Feature Films* I highly recommended that all of you directors take acting classes. Learn the skills of acting (and not with a bunch of directors who are dabbling in the acting arena, but with real, professional actors). I'm off on this tangent now because this 'trick' won't work at all if you have zero acting skills. And you thought you could become an effective director without them. That's like wanting to be a symphony conductor but never learning to play an instrument, or a football coach and never actually playing the game. You want to be an effective director. Learn acting, and learn writing. Immerse yourself in the two most important worlds of storytelling (story and performance). Remember, writers and actors can tell stories without you, but you can't do it without them. Get your feet wet. Test your skills. Develop an understanding and appreciation for the craft.

Let's assume that you have been spending the past few years developing your writing and acting skills and you are fairly decent as an actor. Good. Now you can consider this technique. When a writer (or anyone) hears a script read, they are not only hearing the dialogue, but they are hearing the inner life of the character that is generated by the text mixed with the projection and life experience of the reader. It's very powerful and often very convincing, even if it is not what the writer had in mind. Nothing like a powerful, heartfelt performance to convince anyone that there is a very specific inner life existing within the character.

You are working with the writer on the script and there are those niggling little points of disagreement that you can't seem to get around. Perhaps you, the director, are having a bit of trouble articulating what it is you see, feel or want concerning certain characters or scenes. This is not uncommon.

Many of us can't quite find the words to express what is in our imagination. But often we can hear it. As we read it to ourselves we hear the rhythms and tones and inflections that reveal the inner life of the characters. Let's say it is a specific scene and you feel strongly that there is a deep level of suspicion and distrust between the characters. It's not really written that way. It's clear to you that this may not have been the writer's intention. But you are convinced that this aspect of the relationship needs to be explored.

TRICK: THE DIRECTOR AND WRITER READING

Here is a simple and straightforward way to bring the writer to your way of thinking. Offer to read the scene, you and the writer. Simply say, "Let's read this scene and see what happens." The writer may not be much of an actor, but that is not a problem. He will read the part (perhaps poorly) with the inflections, attitudes and intentions as he sees and feels them. This will be clear. But what are you doing? You are going to read your role in such a way that the writer will suddenly sit up and hear something new and may even be forced to adjust his reading in response to you.

And you can even take it a step further (more reason for those acting classes) and allow yourself to embody the character physically, moving around, engaging in activities and behavior. Now the writer is in the presence of the character you envision. Once the reading is done, ask the writer what he thinks. Not about your performance (this is not an acting critique), but of the relationship between the characters. Take it a step further and ask the writer what it felt like to be in the scene and how he (as the other character) feels about your character.

If this doesn't begin to persuade the writer to consider your vision for this character, you can take it one more step. Tell the writer how it felt to be your character. For those few moments you embodied the character and the character spoke through you. One terrific thing about feelings is that they can never be wrong. They are just feelings. If you say:

> "You know, when I was engaged in that scene with you I felt distrust and suspicion. I was really surprised. I hadn't expected that." (Of course you had, that was what you were going for.) "Wow. You probably felt that too, I imagine. What do you think? Do you think that it's there?"

By this point you are now heavily into the discussion of this new aspect of this relationship. And the writer, most likely, is seeing this as a discovery and not an imposed idea from the director.

TRICK: WHEN THE ACTORS READ IT
I HEARD SOMETHING NEW

This trick is as old as the hills. Or at least it goes back as far as the first faltering steps in the relationship between someone calling himself a writer and someone else taking on the role of director. Because it is that old and that pervasive and powerful you do have to be careful because it can backfire. You'll see what I mean in a minute.

You're working with the writer and you have found yourself at an impasse on certain issues relating to character or relationships between characters. You see it one way and the writer sees it another way. In your infinite wisdom you know it is time to bring in the big guns, the cavalry — the actors. You casually mention: "Perhaps it would be good to get a new perspective on the material by hearing it read out loud by some actors." The writer also thinks this is a good idea because the writer is convinced that in the hands of professional actors, the writer's intentions (and visions) will become clearer. Problem is, you are thinking the same thing: With professional actors, the writer will finally see things go your way.

So, you get the actors, do a little rehearsal, and you have your reading. The focus here is not on the text or the reading. It must be on the subtext. Concentrate on what you hear and feel coming from the actors. And you must get your writer to do the same thing.

Important: if you go into this process certain that this reading will convince the writer of the wisdom of your vision — forget it. We are playing with fire here. The fire is the actors. Assuming that they are truly talented and bring honesty to every moment, then the subtext that you hear and feel is what is really going on.

Side note: There's a big wild card here — rehearsal. You have several choices and each choice has a level of security and a level of risk.

First, you could have no rehearsal at all. You just cast the characters as best you can, give them time to become familiar with the material, and then you and the writer sit and listen to them read it together for the first time. The risk here is that you may not get what you want. In fact, the reading could easily support the writer's point of view. The security is that you could assert that the casting was off, the actors weren't prepared enough, and with more rehearsal, etc. It's a weak argument.

Second, you rehearse a little bit with the actors (writer present or not present, your choice) and you guide them in the direction that you are going, thereby giving yourself a bit more assurance that you will be able to sway the writer in your direction.

Third, you rehearse a lot and bring the script to a finely tuned level of performance (ideally without the writer) so that the actors' performances are confidently supporting your vision. With the second and third choices, of course, you could be accused (accurately) of stacking the deck in your favor. The bigger risk is that during rehearsals you discover that your ideas aren't holding water. If this happens, then the exercise has been truly successful and beneficial.

If during the reading you realize that the performances are actually supporting the writer's vision and not yours, don't panic. See it for what it is. This is why you have to be careful when you bring in third parties. You truly have no control over them, even if you have rehearsed extensively. Genuine subtext has a way of coming through regardless.

What you see and hear in the actors' performances is only part of the benefit of this process. What needs to be explored are the actors' experiences and points of view. Talk to them after the reading. They have a unique perspective (different from yours and from the writer's). They experience the characters from the inside. Listen to them, question them, and suggest other possibilities.

Now we are into the collaboration process. Remember that other book? *Directing Feature Films*? Well, it's time to read it again.

However the reading goes, whatever comes out of the performances will be of enormous benefit to your process. Embrace it.

Cutting a Scene, Character, or Event

When we're considering major surgery on a script, we're entering into dangerous territory. Let's assume that you want to remove what we will lovingly call the "offensive material." It's one thing to shift dialogue, alter behavior, change locations or suggest specific staging details within a scene. But it is totally something else to suggest to a writer that we cut a scene, character, or event. This writer labored hours on the development of this particular element in the script and most likely will be very reluctant to let it go. She sees how it should work in the story, she feels how it should work, or at least knows how it was meant to work.

Now, you could just face this issue straight on and tell the writer what you want cut and hope that you can duck quickly or leave the room before the explosion happens. Or you can practice sleight-of-hand. The goal with this trick is, once again, to get the writer to come up with the idea of excising the material in question. Now you get to really test your skills. This is close-up work. The observers are hovering over you, watching your hands. They know what you are doing and they are just waiting for you to slip or make a mistake.

TRICK: MICROSURGERY

This is a multiple-stage trick. So take one careful step at a time.

Step One: Praise
First, praise the offensive material. That's right, praise the offensive material. This is right in line with 'express enthusiasm.' There is nothing like softening the resistance of the writer (and later we will see how this works with the actor) by spreading a little genuine praise (Novocaine) on the area where the incision is about to be made.

Let's say it's a character you want removed. The reason you want her removed is that she is really inappropriate for this story and this film. She's very colorful (was probably inspired by the writer's mother or aunt) and she dominates every scene she is in. You can tell by the way the writer talks about this character and by the writing itself, that this is a cherished character, one that will leave kicking and screaming. So you need to proceed carefully. Praise the character.

> "You know, I think this is one of the best characters you have ever written. She is powerful, independent, unpredictable, mysterious and engaging. Too bad she isn't the protagonist. She really deserves her own story."

You do see where this is leading, don't you?

Step Two: More Praise

That's right, you have to hit the writer with another positive (see "2+1+1" later in this chapter). It's not a one-two punch; it's a one-two stroke. Something like this:

> "And you know, she dominates every scene she is in to the point that I am more interested in her than I am our main characters. Now I'm not saying this is a problem..." (don't you just love disclaimers?) "...but the fact is we have to either redesign and strengthen the other characters and bring them up to her level or we have to back her off, reduce her. Now, I don't like the idea of weakening this character (I'd prefer to kill her) and we might lose the essence and integrity of the other great characters you have created (keep the praise going) if we tried to bring them to her level."

Step Three: The Invitation

Then, like any accomplished magician, you go right into silence. Silence is powerful. In an environment of negotiations, discussions, creative outbursts and collaborative conflicts, silence creates a void, an opening, and an invitation. You hit the writer with silence at this point and she will feel the need or obligation to fill it. And that is exactly what you want. We are tricksters, masters of sleight-of-hand. Our goal is to get our audience (in this case the writer) to arrive at the conclusion we have already embraced. The silence is the invitation. In the silence we are saying:

> "You know, it will be a lot less painful if you just come up with the idea and decide to do it yourself than putting yourself through the pain of having me insist on 'killing' this character."

But of course you don't say that. You wait. And let's assume she doesn't bite. She hangs in and hangs on and we have to go for the kill.

Step Four: The Kill

> "Okay, why don't we just remove the character from the script so we don't do damage to her or to the other characters and see how well the story can exist without her. You know, sometimes you take one element out of a story and suddenly the entire story shifts and gets stronger in response. That could happen here."

Step Five: The Salve

> "But I want you to hold onto this character because she is phenomenal. I truly think you are doing a disservice to her by making her a secondary character in this story. You really know this woman, there's something inside you that wants to honor this woman. Let's give her a story of her own. I see another script developing already."

Surgery is done. The patients (both the script and the writer) are now in post-op and have to be treated with kid gloves. But the recovery will lead to a stronger script (or so you assume). And if it doesn't, and it is clear that the removal of the colorful character destroyed the story, then you and the writer have learned a valuable lesson. Not just in diplomacy, writing, and collaborating, but about the script itself. This surgery may have revealed other weaknesses and strengths in the material and that is always a good thing. And, if you come to the decision that the colorful character will have to be returned to the story, then you get to do that magnanimously by saying:

> "You were right. I was wrong. Thank you for hanging in there and thank you for trying it my way. Let's put her back."

TRICK: CLAIMING INSANITY AS A MEANS TO AN END

Let's say none of these elusive or indirect approaches are working. Or perhaps you feel that you don't want to take the time to manipulate or seduce the writer into compliance. You know what you want. You are pretty sure that the writer is going to hate the idea and you want to get to it as quickly as possible and either get it done or move on. But you really like the idea because it is creative or bizarre or original. So, time for another trick: The self-deprecating 'I must be insane' approach, which is designed to shield you from a frontal assault.

Let's say you are discussing our story about the couple driving cross-country in the car owned by the stranger. You've read the script many times and at the end of the second act (dangerous territory because too many scripts falter and fall apart at this point) you know the story is in trouble. The man and woman are at each other's throats, they have a thousand more miles to drive together and they are running out of money. But there is nothing that seems to be raising the stakes, and you know you need the stakes raised as you go into the third act or the audience will get restless. So you say:

> "Okay, here's a truly insane idea. You have to forgive me because sometimes my mind just goes into weird places. So, I'll just throw it out there and you can shoot it down and we'll be done with it."

You know that if you stopped right here you have most likely ignited the curiosity in the writer to such a degree that he will beg to hear this 'insane' idea. You might even play the old 'passive/aggressive trick' and say:

> "No, forget it. It's truly insane and unworkable and would most likely destroy the entire story."

Have you noticed how all of the objections to the idea (that you haven't stated yet) have already been put on the table? Very clever. It's hard to attack an idea when the person presenting the idea has already voiced all of the objections. So the writer continues to insist and you, reluctantly of course, give in and say:

> "What would happen at this moment if the man who owned the car showed up? I know, I know, stupid idea. The story really isn't about him and he's never been in the story at all except through a few phone calls, and now having him in the story when they are over one thousand miles from their destination and running late and no money would really confuse everything."

We're covering all of the objections here before the writer even gets to respond. Remember how we used silence in an earlier trick to give the opportunity for the writer to respond? Well, we are doing the opposite here. We throw out the new idea, call it 'insane' and then immediately give all the reasons why it won't work and keep talking and talking. The writer has no opportunity to respond at all and that is the intention. Since he can't really respond, all he can do is think and absorb and consider, and that is precisely what we want him to be doing. And we are watching him as we continue to dismiss the 'insane' idea and give all the objections. Watch him closely and you may see the moment when the pure wisdom of this idea hits him. He's heard the idea and all the objections and problems and then, quite possibly, he sees the upside and how this seemingly 'insane' idea will actually propel us into the third act. Like all the other tricks, there is a roll of the dice here. It may not work. In fact, you may even convince yourself that it was truly an insane idea. And that's okay. Or the writer just may agree with you and enthusiastically embrace one of your objections. And that, too, is okay. The good thing is that the idea is out there and there is always that possibility that it will come back all on its own.

Responding to Rewrites:
A Delicate Dance of Seduction

Express enthusiasm. Yep, again, express enthusiasm. You got your rewrites and for that you should be pleased. Now, read them and express enthusiasm and keep it genuine. Of course they won't be what you thought or imagined or prayed for. But they are rewrites. Your first task here is to honestly assess what you have. What are the strengths, what are the weaknesses? What's new that is unexpected and what is missing? You express enthusiasm for one primary reason — to keep the writer open, flexible, happy, and working. One harsh criticism and you can turn the tap off forever. One genuine compliment or statement of appreciation and the creative juices welling within the writer will keep bubbling.

Then, depending on the next step you want to take in the rewriting process, you can go back to one of the tricks in this chapter. Good luck.

The Script Is Never Finished

First of all, remember one important fact. A script is never finished.

Just the other day while I was working with two writers who have a script in development in our company, I heard one say, "And then the script will be done." I was shocked. I never consider a script finished until the film is locked and released. And only then because there is really no way to go back and keep working on it. A well-known truth: "Films are never finished, only abandoned." Well, I think I feel the same way about scripts....

One last trick before we enter the casting and rehearsal process.

TRICK: 2+1+1

Or: How to make "No" sound like "Yes"
Or: The Negative Sandwich

This is a major sleight-of-hand and takes a great deal of practice. But once mastered, it will serve you well everyday in so many ways.

You're a director and you want to collaborate. You want to collaborate and collaboration invites ideas, thoughts and input from others. You don't want to shut off this flow of enthusiasm but you do need to handle it with grace and aplomb, especially when you have to say "No." The question is: How do you say "No" to someone who has just eagerly made what he or she believes to be a brilliant suggestion? How do you say "No" without doing damage?

It's called **2+1+1**. Simple concept, tricky to do. And is it a 'trick'? Definitely. 2+1+1. Two positives, one negative, and one more positive. Here's how it goes.

A possible scenario: A member of your creative team, Jim (could be a writer, actor, designer, producer, or whatever) comes to you with a suggestion:

> "Hey, wouldn't it be great if John found out during the course of the journey cross-country that he is indeed gay? Wouldn't that be great and funny? And he finds out just as Carol has professed her undying love for him? Wouldn't that be great? And he's thinking that maybe he is more interested in the man who owns

this car than the woman he has been traveling with for the past week. Wouldn't that be great?"

Now, you hear and feel the enthusiasm and the genuine desire to participate in the creative process. You don't want to step on that. You don't want to squash that enthusiasm because who knows — someday this very same person might come up with something truly brilliant. But, as you listen to this current idea you are horrified. It's truly clear that this person has no idea what the story is really about, he has no idea of the development of the characters and the arc of this central relationship. Otherwise he wouldn't come up with such an absurd idea. Time for 2+1+1. It could go something like this:

"Jim, great idea. And I am really impressed with the complexity of the idea and that you are seeing the potential relationships between all the characters."

Okay, that was positive number one. Here comes positive number two.

"Yes, and it would be funny, very funny. I had never thought of such a clever idea."

Second positive delivered, and now time for the one and only negative.

"Unfortunately this great idea can't work with the story and themes we are developing at this time."

And then quickly back to the final positive:

"But please let me know what other thoughts and ideas you have. You apparently have a very fertile imagination and I expect to hear more from you."

And now you are done.

Think about what Jim actually heard. First, he expressed his idea with enthusiasm, passion and pride. Then he heard "great idea," "really impressed," "very funny," and a whole positive tone in reaction to his idea. Then he heard "unfortunately" (which is almost always the best way to begin the single negative response), followed by "can't work," followed by "you have a fertile imagination, let me know what other thoughts you have and thank you." It's a Negative Sandwich. It's a clear, strong and concise negative sandwiched between so much (genuine) positive that the listener is left (usually) with a feeling of gratitude and of having been heard and acknowledged. The negative doesn't sting because of the salves of appreciation and recognition. 2+1+1. Try it. You will be amazed at the results.

Also, don't worry about the recipient knowing what you are doing (and we will discuss this phenomenon a lot more when working with actors). Many times the recipient of the sandwich will know the sandwich is coming, see it coming, and regardless, the sandwich will work. It's that powerful. Most often the recipient will appreciate your making the effort and taking the time to employ the 2+1+1 because you are knowingly softening the blow. The subtext of 2+1+1 is:

> "I do genuinely appreciate your energy and effort and I'm going to have to say 'No,' but I want you to know that I honor you and your intentions and want to keep the channels of communication open."

It's a magical trick and I am constantly amazed at the results and response. Try it out. I think you will be thrilled. And remember, the first time you try it you will probably stumble, but that doesn't matter. It does take practice and it's worth it.

Raising Children

Working with writers and actors is as delicate as raising children. All of you who have raised or worked with children have a distinct advantage over the rest. This is not to imply that actors and writers are immature. Quite the opposite. Most children from infancy to the age of six, seven or eight are open, honest and emotionally available, which makes them quite vulnerable. It is the goal of every actor and every writer to achieve this state. Your ability to handle individuals who are this vulnerable is essential to your creative process. And, yes, I do highly recommend for those of you who have not raised or worked with children to go out and immerse yourself in their world. Volunteer at a daycare center, become a Big Brother or Big Sister, or if you are really courageous, adopt a child. You will be doing yourself a favor.

Now let's go talk to some actors.

For the following exercises you need to select a partner (preferably a writer) to work with you.

EXERCISES:

1. Go online to *www.script-o-rama.com*. Here you will find hundreds of shooting scripts for movies that have been produced.

2. Select a script for a movie that neither of you have ever seen, but a script that you think would interest you. Download it and print it. (You will be using this script throughout this book.)

3. Each of you read the script separately. You as the director and your partner as the writer.

4. Now, read it again, but this time make note of places in the script where you have questions or problems. Do not share these with your partner.

5. Note anything that you think is missing (character, scene, etc.).

6. Make notes on each character, specifically on aspects or behavior of a character that you don't understand or you think are inconsistent.

7. Go back through Chapter One and select specific tricks that you think will help you to address these issues with the writer.

8. Now it is time for you and your partner to get together. You take the role of director and your partner will take the role of the writer.

9. As the director your job is to communicate what you want or need in the script using the various tricks from Chapter One. Your partner will assume the role of the writer and be adamant in the defense of the script.

10. After you have finished, sit with your partner and ask him to share his experiences with you. This is when you will really find out how the tricks are working.

11. This is how you practice these tricks or techniques, in a safe environment.

The Alchemist Hires Some Assistants

Now that we have the writer and the script moving in the right direction, it's time to add some more members to the team.

The actors.

Hmmm… Actors… A curious collection of creative creatures. In Chapters Three and Four we'll get deep into the delicious process of eliciting magical performances, but first we better look at the selection process.

The Casting Process

Remember, we are merely humble storytellers, no different than the poets and bards of ancient times who traveled from town to town, spinning their stories to the delight (and sometimes horror) of their listeners. But we are also filmmakers and we don't get to 'tell' our stories, we get to 'show' our stories, and we need some curious creatures (often known as actors) to portray our characters. And now we are at the selection process. And just like all other stages of bringing this story to life on the screen, we will be employing as much magic and sleight-of-hand as necessary.

Relationships

Relationships are tricky, aren't they? You never know. The person you are just now meeting could end up being a significant person in your life, or not. Could be for five minutes, five years, or the rest of your life. And you know that the way it gets started is significant. Those first moments of connection can deeply influence how the rest of the relationship goes.

Within the casting process we have a great advantage. As each actor walks in we know that we are potentially at the beginning of a significant relationship and we know pretty much how long this relationship could last. And, since we are the director (the Alpha horse) and this poor unsuspecting actor is looking for a job, we are in a great position to get this relationship off on the right foot. Sleight-of-hand? Absolutely.

TRICK: INSTANT RELATIONSHIP

Just like a master magician has to gain the confidence of his audience, a director has to gain the confidence and trust of the actors. And the first meeting is crucial.

The First Meeting

As the actor walks through the door... be there. Don't think you have to establish some 'directorial mystique' by being inaccessible and mysterious. I know a lot of you do this, by instinct or design, and you feel it works for you. You like a display of superiority. You establish a bit of distance and definitely give off the impression of importance and authority. Good. If it works for you, go for it. If you're eventually getting the profound, deep and rich performances from the actors that you so desperately need for your films, fine.

But I know I can't do that. I would know that something is missing. I can feel it at the edges of the relationship… at the line between the known and unknown is lurking some indefinable extra tone/quality/nuance that is the difference between a good performance and a great one. And as the master magicians that we all aspire to be, we want to stimulate every apprentice to the point of greatness. We want what exists at the edge of known and unknown. We want to see the magic that will sparkle and dazzle even our eyes.

Humble Director

So, drop the 'greater than thou' attitude, embrace humility, and allow your aspiring apprentices to feel confident and comfortable and safe. Greet each actor at the door with something like:

> "Hi, I'm the director and I just want you to know what an honor it is to meet you and I look forward to working with you."

The seduction has begun. The relationship has begun. Sleight-of-hand? You bet! Deceptive? Only if you are not sincere. Effective? Absolutely. When was the last time you were greeted with such warmth and acceptance? Remember how it felt? How safe you felt? How respected you felt? That's what we are going for here. We are starting out each and every relationship (whether they last five minutes or the length of the film… or beyond) with this subtext:

> "You are welcome here. I honor and respect you."

Setting the Stage: Creating the 'Safe Zone'

We're starting to develop a very delicate relationship. We know it and the actors know it. And like any good relationship, it will be filled with confidence and a feeling of safety. But 'safe from what?' you might ask. Good question. What's the danger? Why do the actors need to be protected?

Remember when you were a child, five or six years old perhaps, and your parents or guardians would be doing their best to guide you through your day? "Don't touch this. Don't eat that. Stay out of the street. Don't go there, that's not safe. Don't play with that. Stay away from that person." Do you hear all that negative information? Good intentions poorly stated. All we heard then was "don't, don't, don't." Raising children is not easy. And as a good parent knows, there are two basic rules that will work wonders: Create clearly defined boundaries and then, within those boundaries, allow total freedom. That's right, total freedom within well-defined boundaries. This will allow the child to feel safe while also allowing the child to fully express him/herself. This approach works the same way with actors… at any age. Create strict and clear boundaries, then set the actors loose like little wild animals. They'll be happy, free, expressive and feeling so very safe. And like the best sleight-of-hand, both you and the actor know what you're doing. There is an unspoken bond, a contract and an agreement. No different than a parent and a child.

Boundaries
Here are some examples of boundaries you need to create in the casting process:

> "Here's the material I would like you to read."
> "Here's where I'd like you to be (in this chair, in this end of the room)."
> "You will be reading with this actor (the reader)."

Freedom
The freedom part goes something like this:

> "I'm not looking for anything specific here."
> "I just want to see your impulses, your instincts."
> "Surprise me."

You are telling the actor that they have total freedom to create, express, and explore following their own instincts. There will be no judgment. This is precisely what they want and need to allow their creativity to flow. You have removed the cloud of criticism (a vital element in your relationship with actors, a world without criticism) by saying, "I'm not looking for anything specific here. I want to see your impulses and instincts." The freedom that this permission allows is vital, and sadly most directors do not realize it.

When an actor reads a script or even just a scene, she immediately has some preconceived idea of what the director might be looking for. It's usually a cliché or a formulaic rendering of a character or a scene. Most actors will be reluctant to venture very far from that preconceived idea during a casting session because they want to get the job. But if you give them permission to experiment and explore, if you tell them they can journey outside the box and even surprise you — what a gift! And you are really saying to them: "Nothing you do can be wrong," and that is the most crucial gift of all. Now the actor is totally free and that is your goal.

Speed Dating

The casting process is not just you auditioning the actors. Whether or not they can play the role effectively is only a small part of this process. One of the key aspects of casting has to do with relationships — working relationships. You are exploring the potential relationship between you and the actor. And, in a subtle way, it is also the actors auditioning you. Okay, they don't have a vote, but they do have an opinion.

More specifically, will you be able to work with this particular actor and will this actor be able to work with you?

It would be really nice if we could just hand out a questionnaire and get it all resolved in a much simpler way. But that won't work. We need to find more surreptitious ways of extracting this information. Think of this as a form of 'speed dating.' And the better you are at it, the better the results.

The Character of the Actor

First, one thing has to be clear. Most of the actors who are auditioning for you want the job. And those who don't will find some way to sabotage the process so you don't need to worry about them. For the actors who do want the job you have to keep in mind that they are going to do pretty much anything to get it. They will be charming, flexible, available, vulnerable, tough, determined, sure of themselves, etc. Or they might come across as frightened, insecure, aggressive, elusive, difficult, or demanding. So how do you know if this is the real person? In this moment the actors are putting their best foot forward, putting on their best face. In many ways this is who they are when they are under pressure. But who will they be when this pressure is released — only to be replaced by the pressures of rehearsal or production?

Our job is to get behind the façade. We want to meet the real person. And of course there is a trick.

TRICK: CHANGE THE ENVIRONMENT

As long as you remain in the casting and audition process the actor will feel the pressure and respond accordingly. Your job: Change the environment.

Years ago I was casting a play, and was in the final stage of casting the four lead men. This was truly an ensemble piece and I had to be sure that these four men would work well together. Which meant I needed to know more about them. As I was running the final callbacks with about ten different actors it became evident to me that I was not getting beyond their performance abilities and seeing the actors for who they were. In frustration I informed all the actors to just sit in the waiting room and that I would call them when I needed them. After about ten minutes I wandered out into the waiting room to go to the men's room and get a cup of coffee. They were all there — sitting, talking, reading. I could feel a shift of energy as I entered and walked through the room. It was that 'shift of energy' that I wanted to get past. After going to the men's room I returned to the waiting room for my coffee. Again I felt the shift as I entered the room. 'He's in the room' was the feeling. 'The director is in the room and I better be on guard, be attentive.' I got my coffee and then rather than leave the room I sat down. The moment I sat I could feel another shift. 'Now what is he doing?' was the feeling. I asked one of the actors something innocuous, something unrelated to why we were all there. It could have been about the weather or politics or anything. And a conversation began. Some joined in. Others remained more silent, removed. Some made attempts to assert themselves. Others were more reticent, respectful. Some had strong opinions. Others seemed undecided or uncertain. In other words, I was beginning to see who they really were. It was not performing or acting. And if I felt that someone was performing, I assumed that that was part of their personality. It was during this benign conversation over a cup of coffee that I began to formulate my final decisions on how to cast those four roles. Truth is, the casting of this play could not have been more perfect, and I attribute a lot of that to this serendipitous, unplanned moment.

TRICK: A WALK IN THE PARK

You may argue that this is not a trick. And you'd be right. There is nothing devious, hidden, or sleight-of-hand at all here. In fact, it is on the opposite end of the spectrum.

When you are in the process of selecting those apprentices, those collaborators who are going to be instrumental in the creation of your characters, there is a little voice in the back of your head saying, "Do you really want to spend the next three months (six months, a year) with this person?" Bottom line: I realize that no matter how much I audition or observe these actors, I really don't know them. So when it comes down to those final decisions, it is time for "a walk in the park."

It goes something like this.

An actor has been called in for the final callback. Perhaps I have had him read with another actor, often not. The actor comes into the room or my office and all I say is, "Let's go for a walk." And we are up and walking, out of the room, out of the office. If it is in the city we walk through the streets. If it is in the country (where I live and have my office) we will find ourselves climbing up a hillside. Either way, it is just the two of us — walking and talking. The topics of discussion? Almost anything but the film project. Anything. Weather, food, women, men, politics, the environment, cooking, families, parents, birth, death... and primarily ourselves. What am I looking for? Connection, intimacy, safety, trust, honesty. We don't have to agree (best when we don't). We don't have to have had similar experiences. But we need to be comfortable connecting on the most intimate levels. We both must feel safe with each other.

True, this really isn't a trick. There is no way to manipulate such a moment, to make it turn out the way I want. Either the connection and comfort are there, or they are not. Either the trust is felt, or it isn't. This is perhaps the most important part of the casting process.

And now that we are cast and ready to begin work we need to move into the rehearsal process and see what tricks we can employ there.

With these exercises, use the same script that you downloaded after Chapter One.

EXERCISES:

1. Select key scenes from your script for the main characters that you want to use in the audition process.

2. Make specific notes on each character: What you are looking for. Type? Attitude? Characteristic traits?

3. Select a few key tricks from this Chapter that you want to use. (Instant Relationship, Change the Environment, etc.)

4. Call in a few actors (two or three) to read for these parts. Of course they know that you are not doing a real project and only experimenting.

5. Run a casting session. Use the tricks whenever and wherever you can.

6. After you have finished, sit with the actors and ask them to share their experiences with you. This is when you will really find out how the tricks are working.

The Alchemist in Rehearsal

Now you've hired your assistants. Or the way I like to look at it, the sorcerer has a team of apprentices.

Now the real alchemy begins.

First, three very important questions:

1. Why do we go to the movies?
The primary reason that most individuals go to see a movie is the story. You might think it would be genre, actor, director, special effects… but several polls have substantiated that it is the story that is the primary draw. This is very heartening to those of us who are writers, and it should be encouraging to you as a director. Now all you have to do is find or write a good story.

2. Where does the story live?
Your story lives in a very specific place in your film. It is not in the cinematography, the production design, or special effects. It's not in the CGI or graphics. Your story, quite clearly, lives in the characters. It is in their needs, desires, dreams, and actions. It is in their disappointments, pain,

and struggle. Someone coined the phrase 'ordinary people in extraordinary circumstances.' That's perfect. We go to movies to see other people deal with extraordinary circumstances that are not totally within their control. We share these experiences with these characters from the safety of our seat. Without characters there is no story. And without actors we have no characters. So at the center of our story are these characters, portrayed by these actors, selected by you and guided by you. And the audience is paying money and spending time to see these 'ordinary people in extraordinary circumstances.' So, now it is clear how crucial these 'apprentices' are.

3. What is the most important directorial skill?
The answer should be obvious. Your skill at being able to elicit credible, authentic performances from the actors is the most valuable.

Now we're going to look at the alchemist and the actors in the rehearsal process. And as we explore bringing those pages of text to life, we are going to have to dig deep into the bag of tricks. We'll start at the beginning with the first reading.

The First Reading
You'll invite a lot of people besides the actors. You'll have producers, investors, writer(s), cinematographers, designers, editors, and composers — basically whomever you want. The questions are: What do you want to accomplish during this reading? What are your goals?

By now you are well on your way to becoming a master magician, but now, for the first time, you will be doing sleight-of-hand in front of a larger audience. Your goal: Create the illusion that you know what you are doing and that you are in charge and all is well with the world.

Easy to say — not so easy to do.

Especially if you are like me and you feel the gremlins of doubt nibbling away at what little confidence you might have.

THE TRICK: THE CONFIDENCE CON

Note: This trick will serve you well for the remainder of the process of making your film.

What you must do is show complete confidence while admitting that you know nothing. That's right, supreme confidence, total ignorance. It may seem like a contradiction — and it is — but it is actually one of the most powerful directorial tools you possess. It is very attractive and seductive.

Here is an example of how it might work. You are facing twenty or more people at the first reading of the screenplay. They are all looking to you for guidance, inspiration, clarity, and purpose. Inside your gut the gremlins of doubt are having a field day. But in your head there is a voice that tells you this is the most thrilling and frightening moment of your life. And you say something like this:

> "I am excited about this project and the story we are going to tell. I am thrilled with the team we have assembled and know that each of you is going to bring extraordinarily talented gifts to this process. In my head I can see, hear and feel the power of the film we are about to make. And I must admit that at this moment I am a bit nervous and apprehensive, because I have no idea how we are going to achieve all of this."

That's the trick. An honest trick. You are simply saying that you are human, and that as the director you are as flawed and fragile as each one of them. If you can honestly maintain this delicate balance between confidence and uncertainty, you will find that your collaborative artists will shoulder-up beside you, supporting you while guided by you.

The First Reading of the Script

Every person in this room has read the script (we assume). Certain to say that each person has an expectation of how this story will sound, look, play on the screen, etc. Problem is, there is no way to satisfy all of these expectations. Even the actors have their own expectations, and on top of that they are feeling the pressure from all the other expectations in the room. This scenario is primed for disaster. Time for a trick.

TRICK: ERASE EXPECTATIONS

This is another trick that you will use frequently. If you can lower or erase the expectations of your staff, your crew, your actors (and, to an extent, even your audience), you will deflect criticism and avoid disappointment.

Here's how it works.

Make it clear to everyone (especially the actors) that you do *not* expect a performance-level reading. Make it clear to each actor that all you want to hear is the text, the words. I often say, "Don't feel obligated to give a performance of any kind. But if you feel emotionally moved in any direction, let yourself go. Let this be an exploration."

The reason for this request is that you truly do *not* want to hear a performance out of obligation. By 'obligation' I mean a performance that an actor feels is necessary to either please you or to fill the expectations of anyone else in the room. Your job as the director is to remove this self-inflicted pressure from the actors — now and forever.

Also, you are by default informing everyone in the room that there is no room for judgment or criticism. How can you judge or criticize a performance when the actors were requested not to perform?

And there is one very powerful message that you are sending to everyone. And that is: "This is the way we are going to work throughout the process. Exploration. From the first reading to the final take. There is no ideal performance. There is no perfect reading or interpretation. There is only exploration and discovery." More on this later.

TRICK: GRATITUDE AND PRAISE

This is a powerful one that you will be using on a daily basis. And this is so powerful that you can even tell the actors (or anyone else) exactly what you are doing (expose the trick for what it is) and it will still work.

After they finish the reading, say to all the actors: "Thank you. Very good." And mean it!

Remember: Actors will always do the best they can with the information they have. No actor intentionally gives a poor reading or performance. So, after every reading, every performance, every take — throughout the entire process of making this film — always say: "Thank you, very good." Even if you do not like what you just saw or heard. Say it. "Thank you, very good." And mean it!

Thank them for their work, their effort. Acknowledge them. Validate them.

No Criticism

Your job is to keep the actors open and emotionally available at all times. And in order to do this you must create a 'safe space,' an environment that allows them to be free and expressive. And this safe space is a world without criticism.

That's right: No criticism.

"But," you are thinking, "what do I say to an actor when I don't like what they are doing? How do I get them to do what I want if I can't criticize them?"

You can get the actors to do amazing things and give you stunning performances without ever criticizing them. We'll get to this process later in this chapter.

Think for a moment about what criticism does. Forget the actors for a moment. Think of yourself.

Remember the last time someone criticized you for something you had done or not done. Maybe it was a choice you made or an action you took. Maybe it was because you forgot something or simply chose to ignore something. Whatever. You received criticism. Now, recall what happened inside you at that moment. Most likely, if you are like the rest of the human race, your heart seized for a moment, tightened, maybe even skipped a beat. Inside you could feel yourself putting up little protective walls. These walls of defense may have taken the form of rationalization, justification, or explanation. Or maybe they were walls of denial, disconnection, or rejection. Whatever they were — they were walls. And these walls were put into place because in that moment the world did not feel quite as safe as it had previously.

The Actor's Job

Now think of the world of the actor and the job of the actor. The actor's job is more difficult and dangerous than most people realize. The challenge is to mold a believable character from bits and pieces of information mixed with a personal emotion system and range of life experiences. The danger lies in the fact that an actor is tapping into his own emotional network while taking on the persona, problems and passions of a character. He is exposing his own inner life through this character. This creates a high level of vulnerability within the actor. Consequently the actor needs the safest of environments within which to work.

It is your job to create this environment.

One essential aspect of this environment is that there is no criticism. Not from you and not from anyone else on the set or from anyone involved in the production. You need to protect your actors from yourself and everyone else... even from the other actors. No criticism. In fact, in an ideal world, no comments or discussions regarding the actors' work from anyone — except you. You, the director, should be the *only* person who is allowed to talk to the actors about their work. That's ideal and that should be your goal.

Creating this 'safe environment' begins with "Thank you, very good," but goes way beyond that. This aspect of working with actors is crucial and you must not ignore it. Like a mother hen and her chicks, you must be willing to stand at the edge of the rushing traffic, protect your brood, and then guide them safely to the other side.

"Thank you. Very good."

First Rehearsal
This first reading was not a rehearsal, not really. It was a breaking of the ice, a formality. Now the real work can begin. And now the work will proceed most likely without all those other people (producers, designers, editors, etc.), just with the actors. Maybe the writer stays along with a couple of your creative assistants and collaborators. Be mindful of whom you let observe the rehearsal process and why. Keep in mind that the actors need that 'safe environment.' One producer watching from the corner can send waves of criticism and concern just with his body language.

Peripheral Vision
I remember reading once about Bill Walton, the extraordinary basketball player for the Boston Celtics. This article talked about his amazing peripheral vision, how he could see the whole court, all the other players, while still focusing specifically on the goal, the basket. This is a skill that all directors

must develop. We must be able to see and be aware of all that is going on around us while we are relentlessly pursuing our goal of the moment. As you are working with the actors, be aware of all that is going on around you. Be aware of what they are seeing and sensing. Be aware of their very subtle yet revealing reactions to everything. One comment, one piece of behavior from one person can send ripples of doubt, fear or concern through the previously very open and available actor. You have to be aware of this and create those boundaries that will allow your actors to work openly and safely.

Now we're at the first rehearsal, the discussion of characters and the story with the actors and the first readings of scenes.

In *Directing Feature Films* there is a whole chapter on the rehearsal process. I will assume you have read it as we now deal with many of the tricks we directors use in order to stimulate discovery and create performances within the actors.

Point of Concentration (POC)

This is a term that was coined by Viola Spolin in her excellent book, *Improvisation For The Theater* (a 'must read' for all of you). POC identifies what you, the director, should be looking at, or looking for, as you are working with actors.

Improvisation For The Theater is full of exercises, games and improvisations that can bring actors to a whole new level of experience and relationships. Ms. Spolin pinpoints with each exercise precisely what you should be looking for in the actor, in behavior, tone, experience, emotion, etc.

So, we're going to use the same term here — POC. And as we look at each trick it is vitally important that you know where to concentrate, what to look for (or ask for).

Pause and Clip

When actors read a scene, they will, by instinct, follow certain patterns and rhythms. When it is their turn to speak (when they get their 'cue') they will say their line. And of course the actor will wait until the person speaking before them is finished. It's natural. It is the way the script is written, one speech following the other. But this has little to do with the way we converse, the way we hold conversations. We frequently overlap, interrupt, or pause in thought before responding, or even clip off the ending of the other person's statement.

Comfort and Conflict

We go through life with two simple objectives. We seek comfort and avoid conflict. We do this every moment, every day. It is necessary for survival. So when actors read a scene, they will automatically slip into this 'comfort/conflict' mode, which means pick up your cues (say your line when it is your turn) and don't interrupt when another is speaking. Comfort and no conflict.

But, you have to ask yourself, what would happen if we were to override these human instincts? We are making a story that contains drama, human beings in conflict, and human beings outside their comfort zone.

Overriding human instincts and impulses is a big part of our process. We are constantly pushing characters into areas of discomfort and conflict in order to expose the truth of their condition.

TRICK: PAUSE

Simply say to the actor, "After the other actor has finished her line, just count to five, silently to yourself, and then say your line." What you are doing is inserting a pause between the end of one line and the beginning of the response. It is purely mechanical. You are not asking for any emotional content or shift, just the pause.

POC: Watch the actor (watch both actors) as this adjustment takes place. You will see that it has a profound affect on both of them. It doesn't matter that both of them know that this pause has been mechanically inserted. The actress giving the first line will still have to deal with her expectation that the response will come immediately. It's her human instinct and the five-second pause will have impact on her. The actor waiting five seconds to respond will also be dealing with his desire to respond immediately, and as he holds he will feel tension building.

But you must also listen to the line as it is delivered. It will have shifted in tone, intent, and even rhythm. The shift will not be intentional. It will be organic. And even the next line from the actress will be affected.

Continue to run the scene with the actor inserting the five-second pause before he speaks each line. Watch the actors. Listen to the lines. Be aware of the effect this is having on them. The scene will have changed profoundly.

The 'pause' is an insertion of power. The character that suddenly or consistently refuses to acquiesce to the natural rhythm of the scene is actually taking control of the scene. He is forcing the scene into his own rhythm. It is a calm power, a confident power. You will feel this. The actors will feel it. And the lines as delivered will reflect it.

TRICK: CLIP

Also, it is a natural instinct to allow our scene partner to finish speaking before we speak (seeking comfort / avoiding conflict). We attempt to do this in real life (some are better at this than others — I have a tendency to interrupt). And for actors working with scripted material it seems pretty obvious that you should wait for your scene partner to finish before you speak. But what would happen if we were to break that unwritten rule?

Ask your actress to actually 'clip' off the end of the last line of her scene partner. "Don't wait for him to finish. Clip off the last two words." Now run the scene. Again you will see a profound effect on the actors and the scene itself. All of this is triggered by a mechanical change, the clipping of lines of one character by the other.

And this is another assertion of power. It is not the relaxed, confident power of pausing, but rather a restless, aggressive, and impatient power.

The Release

At the moment these techniques are being used without regard to character, objectives, or content of the scene.

Once the actors have had the experiences of both pausing and clipping, it is time to release them. This means remove the rules. Take away the arbitrary demands and let them use either Pause or Clip (or not) whenever they want, as a way of attempting to fulfill the objectives of the character.

POC: As you listen to the pausing or clipping you will hear and feel that it works better at different times for different reasons. And the actors will certainly feel it.

Activities: Independent, Dependent, and Continuums

No matter how large or small, every character is always involved in some activity. It could be something as simple as reading, ironing, or watching television, or as complex as blowing up a building. Regardless, it is an activity.

A **dependent activity** is one that is directly related to the content of the scene.

An **independent activity** is one that is not directly related to the content of the scene.

Imagine a scene where a husband and wife are arguing about whether or not to take a vacation in Hawaii. The husband is poring over the bank statements, checking their finances to see if they can afford such an expense. This is a dependent activity because it directly relates to the content of the scene. But the wife washing the dishes would be an independent activity because it has no connection with the content of the scene.

The engagement of a character in an activity (dependent or independent) is a powerful tool and opportunity for the director. Since one of our primary goals is to reveal the subtext within the scene (see subtext later in this chapter) we can trigger or reveal that subtext through our use of these activities.

TRICK: BREAK THE CONTINUUM

An activity in a scene is a 'continuum.' Here is the dictionary definition:

> *Continuum:* a link between two things, or a continuous series of things, that blend into each other so gradually and seamlessly that it is impossible to say where one becomes the next.

I use the term here to describe an activity that is intended (by the character) to continue at the same rate, rhythm and intensity until completed. The washing of dishes, the reading of financial reports, the folding and filing of papers, are all continuums. It is not the activity that is primary here; it is the breaking of the continuum, the alteration in the rhythm, intensity, or even the total cessation of the activity that is significant. How a character is engaged in an activity, or how that engagement changes, will reveal what is going on inside the character.

Example:

Let's use our hypothetical scene of the husband and wife discussing (and perhaps arguing about) their upcoming vacation. She wants to go to Hawaii and he wants to go to a golf tournament in Utah. The scene is set in their kitchen. The husband is at the kitchen table going over bank statements and reviewing their finances. The wife is at the kitchen sink, washing the dishes from dinner.

At the beginning of the scene the husband brings up the finances, holding up a bank statement (this makes it clear that his activity is related to the content of the scene). The wife is scrubbing a plate, but when she hears the words "Can't afford Hawaii," *she stops scrubbing*, she almost freezes as the husband keeps rambling on about their financial status. She *resumes scrubbing* the plate with renewed energy when he has finished his argument. For a few moments she says nothing (according to the script she has the next line). So we have thrown a Pause in here as well. Then she calmly states, "The last time we went to Utah…" and now we get a slice of history. The husband is *neatly folding his bank statements* and placing them in order into his 'Financial Status' file. Her story is seemingly benign until she says, "…and you and your friends played golf every day. Even on the day it rained when you played with what's-her-name." The *file slips out of his hands* and splays on the floor; *she stops her scrubbing*. Silence. The wife *dries her hands on a towel*, walks to the splayed papers on the floor that the husband is trying to retrieve. She kneels down and *retrieves the last few pages*. As she hands them to her husband she simply says, "We can't afford another Utah." The husband is left *holding the papers, frozen.* The wife returns to the dishes and calmly *begins scrubbing and cleaning.*

Now let's look at the scene and what was revealed by the activities.

1. When the husband says, "Can't afford Hawaii," this breaks the wife's washing activity. And when a continuum is broken, the line that triggered the break will resonate (echo) in the audience's mind, and in the mind of the actress. The words "Can't afford Hawaii" have triggered something deep inside the wife to the point that she has to cease her activity. We are now waiting to discover what that might be.

2. Resumption of washing. When a character resumes the activity is also important. We could have the wife resume washing within seconds of hearing "Can't afford Hawaii," or, as I have chosen here, she waits until the husband has finished his argument. The first choice accentuates her reaction to the line, but her recovery is relatively quick. The second choice creates a greater and lasting tension and makes me feel that there is some history being exposed here, perhaps how accustomed she is to hearing him ramble on about finances and is anticipating the next shoe to drop.

3. The husband neatly folding his financial papers. The way the husband folds and files the papers will tell you volumes about what is going on inside him.

4. The wife stops scrubbing on "what's-her-name." Now, it is important whether she stops scrubbing when she says the line or after she hears the file papers hit the floor. The first: she is stopping to see if there is a response. The second: she is stopping when

she gets the response. Both are totally valid. Each one reveals a slightly different aspect of the wife. And if she resumes scrubbing after she has confirmed the response, this 'closing of the window' makes her behavior a statement.

5. The husband's dropping of the file on "what's-her-name" is one of the most powerful and telling uses of the breaking of a continuum. The wife simply alludes to a person and the husband drops the file. You can feel the volumes of history (spoken and unspoken) in that moment.

6. The wife, abandoning her activity (washing dishes) and drying her hands is both metaphorical and symbolic. And as she retrieves the pages from the floor, for the first time engaging in his activity, she takes control of the scene. And at this moment she makes her final statement: "We can't afford another Utah." The argument or debate is over. She is literally and figuratively handing him back his ammunition.

7. The fact that the husband doesn't move and is left holding the papers while the wife returns to scrubbing the dishes reveals more about how much the husband lost in the argument and how much the wife gained than words could possibly express.

Seems like a lot of analysis and description for a trick, doesn't it? True, it is a lot. And as we continue to plunge into the world of these tricks you will see that the effect is running deeper inside the character and revealing deeper truths. So for our intentions at the moment (me writing this book and you reading it) we need to be very clear about what these tricks are doing and what they are revealing.

And when you look at this trick, it is rather simple. Here are the directions you are giving:

- When he says, "Can't afford Hawaii" — stop washing the dishes.

- Resume washing once he has finished his speech.

- Fold your paper here. You are done.

- Stop washing when you say "what's-her-name."

- Drop papers on "what's-her-name."

- Dry your hands after the papers hit the floor.

- Try to pick up your papers.

- Pick up his remaining papers. Hand them to him on your line "We can't afford another Utah."

- Just sit still, holding the papers.

- Go back to washing the dishes.

Those are simple instructions. Easy to do. And easy to repeat — take after take.

The trick is that each adjustment in the activity will trigger an emotion in the character and in the audience. We are not triggering emotions with emotions, but with behavior.

POC: Now you have to be the innocent and naïve 'audience' member. By innocent and naïve I mean that you have to 'forget' the tricks you have inserted, you have to 'forget' what you are attempting to do. You have to innocently watch the scene. This is one of the most difficult aspects of directing, as we are attempting to override our own projections that will try to convince us that we are indeed seeing the results we so passionately desire.

Watch the actors. Allow yourself to see and feel what they are experiencing as they move through the minefield of this scene. Watch as they adjust to the breaks and resumptions of the activities.

And ask them. Let the actors tell you what they were truly experiencing during the scene. If the emotions and reactions you are observing, and the emotions and reactions the actors are feeling, are exposing the subtext you imagined or desired, then you are going in the right direction. Congratulations.

Staging Tricks During Rehearsal

We did a long discussion of staging in *Directing Feature Films*, but now we will look at how staging tricks during rehearsal can trigger the performances you are looking for.

In your first readings of a scene (or even of the entire screenplay) you and the actors will probably be sitting at a table, scripts laid out in front of you. Sort of the student position, as I like to call it. You are all ready to explore, analyze, discuss, and debate. And for a short time this will be fine. Fine as long as you want everyone to stay in the student mode. But the truth is, this staging (and it is staging) is most likely not helping the actors in their pursuit of the characters. In fact (unless they are playing students sitting at a study table), it is working against them. It is an obstacle.

But it is still early in the process and you really don't know enough about these characters and the scenes to leap into performance staging.

Staging for Rehearsal vs. Staging for Performance

The rehearsal process is exploration and discovery, trial and error. The performance process is delivery. So staging for rehearsal is intended to trigger exploration, discovery, and to stimulate the creative imagination.

The following are three simple staging tricks that can be used in the rehearsal process while you are still reading the scene.

TRICK: CHANGE THE SEATING ARRANGEMENT

Move the actors away from their comfortable positions at the table and see what happens. There is a basic human (and actor) instinct to want to see the person with whom you are talking. Seek comfort — avoid conflict. As soon as we begin to put obstacles in the way of that desire, powerful emotions will be triggered.

1. Back to Back

This may seem extreme, placing two characters back to back. But just try it and you will see amazing results.

- First, they can't see each other, so there is an intensi- fied need to connect.

- Second, they can feel the proximity of each other (depending on how close you have placed them), so there is a heightened sense of intimacy, and perhaps danger.

- **POC:** Watch their body language. Watch their faces. Since they can't be seen by their scene partner, you will begin to observe expressions that reveal what is going on inside.

2. One Behind the Other

- You know the feeling when someone is behind you, looking at you, talking to you. Puts you on edge.

- And you also know the feeling of being that person. A feeling of power.

- Now you are playing with the power dynamics in the scene.

- **POC:** Watch the actors. See how they instinctively respond. You are now inserting tension and conflict into the scene.

3. One Direct, One Profile

Seat them close to each other — one looking off toward some distant object while the other faces the first actor directly.

- **POC:** Watch the actor who is staring off. He will experience a curious tension between being observed and being able to see the other actor in his peripheral vision.

- The actor looking directly at him will most likely feel more power, more control.

Once you understand and experience the sleight-of-hand you are doing here you will be encouraged to experiment.

4. Move an Actor, Read Again

POC: During the reading, watch the actors. See how these new positions are impacting them. Be aware of what you are seeing and feeling. Then, following the reading, ask the actors what they were experiencing. Make mental notes of how each 'trick' triggered new feelings, new emotions, and new sensations.

Now you are beginning a very important part of the *Bag of Tricks* process, experimenting with and developing your own specific tricks.

Let's move on to some larger and bolder moves.

TRICK: CHANGES IN SPACE

We all have areas of comfort around us. We know how we feel when people are either too close or too far away. It causes tension and pressure, perhaps even anxiety or restlessness. Either way, we feel a bit outside our comfort zone.

Changing the distance between the actors and even the location within the room will stimulate emotional responses that may help us uncover the subtext of the scene.

I'll give you some examples, but please feel free to experiment.

Staying with our scene of the husband and wife discussing Hawaii vs. Utah.

Leave the husband at the table (where you've been reading) and have the wife stand in the doorway to the room, leaning against the frame. Now just read the scene.

POC: Your job is simply to listen to the changes in the reading. They will be there, guaranteed. The wife will most likely feel more secure and in control standing in the doorway. The husband most likely will feel less secure being alone in the middle of the room, especially if he has his back to his wife. Understand that I am only projecting what I believe they will feel. I could be wrong, that's fine. What is important is how they do feel, the real feelings that are generated.

This is how you begin to understand and take control of the staging process. Staging is one of your most powerful tools. Respect it. Learn it.

Now switch the positions. Put the wife at the table and the husband in the doorway. You'll have a totally different scene, different feelings, and a different relationship.

Put one character outside, in another room — the scene will change.

Put one character in a chair without the table — the scene will change.

Put one looking out of the window — new scene.

Now you are getting the idea.

But let's focus on what this trick really is.

Obstacles and Staging

Obstacles, as we know, are the great defining aspects of characters and of the scene. As directors we get to play with obstacles. We add them, remove them, increase them, diminish them, and manipulate them. This rehearsal staging is simply playing with very subtle, but powerful, obstacles. You don't need to discuss them or define them. They are there automatically. Here are some that we have suggested:

- Not being able to see your scene partner.

- Feeling that your scene partner is too close or too far away.

- Feeling isolated or abandoned in the middle of a room.

- Feeling disconnected because your scene partner is in another room.

- Feeling the power of observing your scene partner, who can't see you.

- Feeling disconnected because you are watching another scene through a window.

POC: Each one of these will trigger genuine emotions within the actor as they are reading the scene. These are emotions with which they will struggle. These are emotions that you may decide need to be part of the characters' experiences.

And then if you begin exploring independent activities in conjunction with your rehearsal staging, you can suddenly find a whole range of subtextual experiences that bring new insights into your scene.

The World of Subtext

As we discussed above, one of our primary goals as directors (and actors) is to reveal the subtext in a scene. Sounds simple, but it is not. First, there is no one (not even the writer) who really knows what the subtext is. It is totally open to interpretation.

Subtext is running inside each of us all the time. Voices in our head keep telling us what we really think, fear, desire, etc. It's never silent in there. The same is true for the characters in our stories. They each have a constant stream of subtext. The only problem is, it isn't written in the script, so we have to find it.

Definition of Subtext

Remember, subtext is the unspoken, that which the character feels, fears, wishes or dreads and desires to speak, but for some reason can't or won't. And there are many layers or levels of subtext. The deeper you go, the more you dip into the forbidden and dangerous. It is a bottomless ocean of feelings, desires, dreams, dreads, and fears. There is no end in sight.

As with staging for rehearsal, we can simply experiment, insert a variety of subtexts into the scene, and just see what happens.

Remember, we are often not sure of the results we want (in fact, it is best if we have no clear idea of the 'results' we're seeking). What we will be doing in many of these explorations (using the tricks in this book) is merely experimenting, seeing what happens, and using as a barometer our own emotional reaction to the results.

Let's take a look at a scene first before we begin playing with subtext.

From
JUST A RUMOR
by Mark W. Travis

The story so far: Walter and Harriet are a happily married couple, two children, beautiful home, and a housekeeper named Helga. Walter runs a big advertising company and Harriet is a freelance interior designer.

Walter is brash and arrogant and charismatic, and this combination often gets him into trouble, like it just did today. He cleverly put a major client, Mr. Tepelmann, in his place in front of a large group of employees in a conference room. It made Walter look very good, but made Mr. Tepelmann look very bad. Mr. Tepelmann, in a private conversation, just threatened Walter with the potential loss of his business.

Harriet is a brilliant, impulsive designer. Uneducated, untrained, but with instincts that are impressive. Problem is, her clients often know more than she does, which immediately causes her to feel inadequate and insecure. Sylvia, wealthy and powerful, just made artistic references regarding Harriet's work that Harriet didn't understand at all. These were intended as compliments, but received as criticisms.

Note: Harriet and Walter, in order to have time alone together, have rented a private beach house. They meet there two or three times a week. It is the only time when they can be quiet, alone, and talk privately with each other.

```
EXT. LOS ANGELES STREETS
Walter driving his Black BMW. No MUSIC
playing. He's on his phone, it's RINGING
through the speaker system.
```

                    WALTER
        Come on, come on, come on. Answer.

Finally, Harriet answers:

                    HARRIET (O.S.)
            What?

                    WALTER
            I need to see you.

Intercut with:

INT. WHITE SUBARU
Harriet, in way too much Traffic.

                    HARRIET
            Now? You need to... Where?

                    WALTER
            The Beach House.

                    HARRIET
            Look, we can't. It's too late,
            it's way too much... That Goddamn
            bitch!

Walter cringes.

                    HARRIET (CONT'D)
            She thinks she's so goddamn
            smart... Ming Dynasty! Where does
            she get off telling me that she
            knows what I'm doing when I
            have no idea what I'm doing?

                    WALTER
Can we not do this?

                    HARRIET
Do what?

                    WALTER
This yelling on the phone
stuff. This isn't talking,
Harriet, it's yelling. Harriet,
we promised each other...

                    HARRIET
But I'm scared, Walter. Why do
I always feel... what the hell is
it with this traffic?

                    WALTER
That's why we have the Beach
House, Harriet. Meet me in...

                    HARRIET
I can't. I can't. I was ready
to talk this morning and all
you wanted was sex. Now you
have a new problem and I can't
just drop everything... and when
am I gonna stop feeling so
insecure? I gotta go home.

                    WALTER
Just tell Helga to take care of
the kids.

```
                        HARRIET
            No, Hope needs me, I promised...


                        WALTER
            I need you.


                        HARRIET
            I can't talk anymore. I can't
            do it anymore. I gotta go.
```

And she hangs up.

Walter pulls over to the side of the road and stops. The Beach House sits in front of him in the growing darkness.

Harriet sits in stalled traffic as the sun sets behind her.

Okay, now you have read the scene. This scene, like almost every scene, is jam-packed with subtext. But of course, all the script gives us is the behavior and the dialogue. We need to find the subtext.

Below are two major subtext exercises, designed to stimulate, provoke, and hopefully unearth the emotional energy that is under any scene.

The first exercise (trick) is in four parts/phases.

TRICK: SUBTEXT INTERJECTION

Phase 1: The Line After
Look at the scene (we'll use the scene above as an example). Select a single line of subtext for each actor. Ask yourself (or ask the actor) what the character would really like to say in this scene, but for some reason can't or won't.

Here are some options:

Walter:	Harriet:
– "Please talk to me."	– "Don't talk to me."
– "I'm scared."	– "I am so pissed off."
– "I'm so angry with myself."	– "I'm scared."

These subtext choices are very simple, very direct, and quite clearly suggested by the text.

All you have to do is pick one for each character and the instructions are simple. They are to say their subtext line out loud at the end of each speech they make. Now the subtext lines become the cue lines for the other actor. Let's imagine that you have chosen: Walter — "Please listen to me," and Harriet — "Don't talk to me."

Here is what the scene will sound like (with the interjected subtext in bold):

EXT. LOS ANGELES STREETS
Walter driving his Black BMW. No MUSIC playing. He's on his phone, it's RINGING through the speaker system.

             WALTER
   Come on, come on, come on. Answer.
   Please listen to me.

Finally, Harriet answers:

             HARRIET (O.S.)
   What? **Don't talk to me.**

             WALTER
   I need to see you.
   Please listen to me.

Intercut with:

INT. WHITE SUBARU
Harriet, in way too much Traffic.

> HARRIET
> Now? You need to... Where?
> **Don't talk to me.**

> WALTER
> The Beach House.
> **Please listen to me.**

> HARRIET
> Look, we can't. It's too late, it's
> way too much... That Goddamn bitch!

Walter cringes.

> HARRIET (CONT'D)
> She thinks she's so goddamn smart...
> Ming Dynasty! Where does she get off
> telling me that she knows what I'm
> doing when I have no idea what I'm
> doing? **Don't talk to me.**

> WALTER
> Can we not do this?
> **Please listen to me.**

> HARRIET
> Do what? **Don't talk to me.**

                    WALTER
This yelling on the phone stuff.
This isn't talking, Harriet, it's
yelling. Harriet, we promised each
other... **Please listen to me.**

                    HARRIET
But I'm scared, Walter. Why do I
always feel... what the hell is it
with this traffic? **Don't talk to me.**

                    WALTER
That's why we have the Beach House,
Harriet. Meet me in... **Please listen
to me.**

                    HARRIET
I can't. I can't. I was ready to
talk this morning and all you wanted
was sex. Now you have a new problem
and I can't just drop everything...
and when am I gonna stop feeling so
insecure? I gotta go home.
Don't talk to me.

                    WALTER
Just tell Helga to take care of the
kids. **Please listen to me.**

                    HARRIET
No, Hope needs me, I promised...
Don't talk to me.

                    WALTER
I need you. **Please listen to me.**

                  HARRIET
I can't talk anymore. I can't do it
anymore. I gotta go. **Don't talk to
me.**

And she hangs up.

Walter pulls over to the side of the road
and stops. The Beach House sits in front of
him in the growing darkness.

Harriet sits in stalled traffic as the sun
sets behind her.

This scene has changed, dramatically. And all we have done
is interject one line of subtext for each character.

When you have the actors do this exercise, something else
will happen. The speaking and hearing of the subtext lines
will have a dramatic and unavoidable impact on both of
them.

A few points about subtext and this exercise:

1. There is subtext under every line we speak or hear in
   our daily lives. Sometimes dramatic and disturbing,
   often benign, sometimes playful, sometimes hurtful,
   always revealing.

2. These lines of subtext are usually never spoken out
   loud, but they are most often felt or sensed by others.

3. If and when we speak these subtextual thoughts out
   loud (letting them become text), we (and our listener) will feel the full impact of them. One reason
   we don't express them is because we fear feeling the
   full emotional impact of the statement.

4. If and when we hear the true subtext of another we will also feel the full impact of those thoughts and feelings on us. We are no longer able to dismiss or ignore them.

5. In this exercise (Subtext Interjection) we are allowing (forcing) the characters to speak and hear these hidden thoughts and feelings, thereby intensifying the veracity and impact of the chosen subtext.

Phase 2: New Subtext Lines

Now pick a new line of subtext and repeat the above. Find a new line for each character that is significantly different from the first, perhaps deeper or in a whole new territory. You might use: Walter — "I'm angry," and Harriet — "I'm scared."

POC: Listen to and be aware of the changes in the scene, in the characters. And even though the subtext line remains the same throughout the scene you will notice that it works better after certain lines than it does with others. Often it will feel startlingly accurate, and frequently it will feel inappropriate. You will also notice how, the more you and the actors explore this technique, the delivery of the subtext line will change depending on where you are in the scene. These are the elements you have to listen to. They reveal what is going on inside the actor/character.

Pick a third subtext. By this point the actors will most likely be making suggestions or requests. Once you have done this exercise with three different subtexts you are read for Phase 3.

Phase 3: Actor's Choice

Now that the actors have had the experience of three lines of subtext (with each impacting the scene and their experiences in a different way), have them read the scene and instruct them to select any one of those lines of subtext to go after each speech.

You are now returning the controls to the actors and they will by instinct select the most appropriate subtext for each moment in the scene. They may even begin sliding off the three options and create their own, and this is fine. What is important now is that you and the actors have explored and developed one way of openly expressing the subtext of the scene. Most actors, once they get a taste of this process, will embrace the opportunity to let those inner feelings and thoughts explode into the scene.

Phase 4: No Subtext Interjection

That's right. Now you take it all away and ask the actors to just read the scene as written. No subtext spoken at all. And here is what will happen to them. After having experienced the joy (and pain) of expressing what is really going on inside their character, the subtextual feelings are right under the surface and the desire is still there to speak them out. This is exactly what you want. Now the subtext is actually driving the scene.

TRICK: SIMULTANEOUS MONOLOGUES

This technique is discussed in detail in *Directing Feature Films*, but it bears repeating here. Once you start tapping into the world of subtext, there are numerous ways of exposing this most vital resource. You are now at the center of the world of the characters; everything emanates from the characters' subterranean world of feelings, thoughts, desires and experiences.

Quite simply, Simultaneous Monologues go like this: Two actors sit and face each other. You, the director, select a topic that is key to each of their characters. Something like: how they (the characters) feel about each other, what they think about sex, money, their mutual friends, children, etc. Naturally each character will have strong feelings on the subject. Then you let them express these feelings to each other (as the characters) in two continuously running monologues. This is not a scene. There is no dialogue. There are two monologues going on simultaneously.

What is the trick here? Good question. Our sleight-of-hand here is to bypass the cognitive process of the actor. We bypass it by overloading it. We almost shut it down completely. We force the actor's brain to take a back seat while the character's brain works overtime.

Try it. Try it with the Walter and Harriet characters above. But remember — the more the actors know about the characters, the better this exercise will work. You are now (like with Subtext Interjection) forcing them into the world of subtext. In Simultaneous Monologues the actors are digging deep into their own inner experiences, feelings and desires, and their knowledge of the characters to mine the 'truth' of their character as best they can.

Variations on Simultaneous Monologues
There are many variations on this Simultaneous Monologue exercise. Here are a few you can try. And feel free to experiment. All good magicians experiment, explore, push the envelope.

Monologue Topics:

- Topics can range from the public (issues or concerns that are known to others), the professional (work related) to the personal (issues just between the two characters) to the private (very individual issues that perhaps the other character doesn't know about).

- The topics assigned could be the same (meaning they each talk about the same issue, feeling, event, etc.).

- The topics could be different. One could be talking about a professional issue while the other is talking about something personal or private, for instance.

Directorial Input:

- Change of topic: At any time you can stop them, give each of them a new topic and have them continue.
  - ☆ **Note:** The less 'down time' there is for the change of topic, the better. You want them to stay in character and not slip out into the analytical or inquisitive area of the actor.

- Stopping One Character: At any time, stop one character from talking (a touch on the shoulder will do this).
  - ☆ This shifts the whole energy. The silent character has to listen to the other. The speaking character suddenly becomes aware that he is being heard clearly.
  - ☆ You can restart the character at any time.

- Events: Change the topic to an event in their past — first meeting, specific argument, first kiss, wedding day, birth of a child, beginning of a partnership, etc.
  - ☆ When working on a shared past event, you can ask them to "build it" — meaning that they have to work together to create the memory of the event. This also means that they cannot deny information being input by the other.

Other Subtext Tricks

Once you have opened up the world of subtext to the actors, there are many variations of all of the above exercises that you try. Each exercise (trick) will reveal new mysteries and possibilities.

TRICK: TEXT VS. SUBTEXT

- Have one actor read the text as written. Allow the other actor to respond with subtext prior to saying her line.

- When she does finally say her line, the first actor can only respond with the text as written.

TRICK: SUBTEXT BEFORE TEXT

- Have both actors respond to the other actor's line with subtext first, eventually followed by the written line of text.

- Each actor must wait until they hear the next line of written dialogue before they can begin to respond.

TRICK: SWITCH

- The actors begin with the text, as written.

- When you say "Switch," they immediately shift to subtext, two subtextual monologues — open and raw — simultaneous.

- Say "Switch" again and send them back into the text. This exercise is obviously under the control of the director. "The Touch" gives the control to the actors.

TRICK: THE TOUCH

Similar to "Switch" except

- The actors sit across from each other, reading the text.

- When one actor (either one) touches the other, they both have to switch to subtext — simultaneous monologues.

- And they have to stay in subtext as long as one is touching the other.

- When the physical contact is broken, they both have to go back to the text.

TRICK: CONTINUOUS SUBTEXT

This exercise (trick) allows for a stream of subtext to come to the surface and be exposed. This is a very difficult exercise for the actors (just a warning) and it takes some practice to be able to tap deeply into that subterranean world.

Here is how it works:

- The actors will read the scene.

- As soon as each actor finishes their first line of dialogue, they go immediately into subtext. But rather than just give one line of subtext, they will speak continuously (another form of Simultaneous Monologue).

- This means that each actor, after the first line of dialogue, will plunge into (and speak out loud) the world of subtext. And continue speaking that subtext until they hear their next cue line.

- Upon hearing their next cue line they will pull out of the subtext (whenever they are ready) and say their next line of dialogue (written text), and then plunge immediately back into the world of their subtext.

You can imagine the cacophony that is going to ensue. It gets wild, chaotic, and dangerous. Not dangerous for the actors, but certainly dangerous for the characters. I suggest you start this exercise out very slowly, let the actors get used to the idea. This switching back and forth between text and subtext is not easy, but its effects are tremendous.

The challenge for the actors is that they have to concentrate on the text (say their lines, listen for the cue lines), switch from text to subtext, and simultaneously really listen to everything their scene partner is saying. It's an enormous strain, an incredible workout.

POC: Listen to and watch everything. Listen to both streams of subtext (which will be going on simultaneously), listen to the lines of text and how they are being affected, watch the physical behavior of both actors as they struggle to reveal subtext while concentrating on their scene partner.

Subtext Wrap Up

By now you should be getting a pretty clear idea of what subtext is and how the revealing of subtext can enhance the scene and the actors' work. You are now in the 'hot spot' of the scene, of the relationship, and of the characters. This is where the sunken treasure lies. This is the gold we have all been seeking. And now you know the magic tricks that can help you to mine this gold.

Staging the Scene Tricks

We have looked at staging in the rehearsal process as a way to help expose the inner life of characters and of the scene. Now we will discuss how staging the scene can take us even deeper.

First, some basics about staging.

Staging is moving the actors in relationship to each other, to the set (location), and to themselves (body language). As you change the body language and physical relationship between the actors, you will automatically trigger emotional responses in the actor. This emotional response is genuine, not manufactured. You will also trigger emotional responses in the audience (viewers) that will likewise be genuine.

As discussed in *Directing Feature Films*, staging is one of the most powerful, useful, efficient (and sadly misunderstood and misused) tools that a director has.

The Power of Staging

Several years ago, when I was directing a play, I was watching one scene and for some reason it really wasn't working well at all. And in that moment it became clear to me that I had three possible ways of solving the problem.

1. I could ask the playwright for a rewrite.

2. I could go back and work with the actors, reexamining the scene, the characters, discussing objectives, obstacles, needs, desires, risks, etc.

3. I could restage the scene.

And it was in that moment that it became so crystal clear to me how powerful the tool of staging really was. Not only was the staging (or restaging) of the scene a possible solution, but also it was very likely that the way I had originally staged the scene was actually the problem.

Do you realize how efficient staging is? Do you realize how quickly you can change the staging, either on a grand scale, or even in a micro moment? And are you aware that these changes will totally alter the impact and experience of the scene?

Staging is strictly mechanical. It is not emotional. When you move or adjust the actors in relationship to each other, to the environment, or to themselves, all you are doing is making simple mechanical adjustments. Make the adjustments and the emotions will follow.

Restaging: An Example

I was running a workshop in Dublin recently. One of the student directors (a fine experienced director) was working on a scene from *Thelma & Louise.* It's a simple scene. The final scene between Louise and her boyfriend, Jimmy. He has just brought her the money she requested (surprising her with his arrival… she requested that he not come) and he has proposed to her. He has even offered to stay with her regardless of the trouble she is in. She has told him nothing except that he can't stay with her and she will "catch up with him down the road." It's a painful scene. Both of them knowing or feeling that it is all over, but neither of them wanting to admit it.

They are sitting at a table. Louise is trying to get Jimmy to leave. Jimmy is trying to assure Louise that he truly cares for her, loves her, trusts her, so that he can leave with as much dignity and self-confidence as possible. At least this is what the actors and the directors had decided. I watched the scene; we all watched the scene. It was good, but something was missing. I kept watching the body language of the two actors. The actress (Louise) was sitting back, relaxed, staring out of the café window, trying to avoid eye contact with Jimmy. The actor (Jimmy) was slouched in his chair, watching Louise. The point is: There was no tension or conflict in the scene because there was no tension in or between the bodies of the two characters.

I asked (through the director) what the two characters wanted. Louise said she just wanted Jimmy to leave. She knew the taxi was arriving soon and he would then have to leave. Jimmy said that he was just trying to say the right things but really wanted to get out of there. As I listened to this I could see that the actors had allowed the characters to physically express where they wanted to be, not where they were. All the tension was gone, everything was resolved.

I asked the actress to sit up straight, turn her body toward Jimmy and look him in the eyes, and to only look away when it gets too painful. I asked the actor to sit up, lean on the table, toward Louise, try to get as close as he could to her and to maintain eye contact as long as possible.

They did as I asked. They ran the scene again.

Now it was a totally different scene. The restaging, the changes in simple body language, suddenly brought the tension and the longing back into the scene. The actors (and director) had allowed themselves to assume positions that reflected their desires (to escape) and I simply put them in positions that were contrary to that. The new positions suggested (and made them feel) the deeper desires to be together and the internal struggles that they were both experiencing.

So what's the trick here? Since it is our natural tendency to seek comfort and avoid conflict, you have to watch the actors and make sure that they are not allowing themselves to find this comfort and safety in their body language. That will be their instinct. Your job is to reinsert the tension and discomfort by simply making a staging adjustment.

Other Staging Tricks

TRICK: CHANGE THE ENVIRONMENT (PHYSICAL)

Every scene in every screenplay starts with a scene heading (or slug line) that describes the location of the scene. Interior or Exterior. It could be a park, a living room, forest, a car, or kitchen… wherever. And then the time of day: Dawn, Day, Dusk, Night, etc.

When the writer wrote this scene he/she selected that location and time of day for a specific reason. But that does not mean you are obligated to keep it as it is. Not at all.

Example #1:
Earlier in this chapter I described a scene between a Husband and Wife and I placed it in the kitchen. She was doing the

dishes and he was going through financial papers at the kitchen table. Imagine that the writer was very specific about this location (the kitchen) and where the characters are placed in the location (kitchen sink and kitchen table). But what would happen if this scene were to take place in the living room? Or the hallway? Or the bedroom? Or the garage? What if it was in the Husband's office? Or in the basement?

All of these locations are in the house: INT. HOUSE. But what if we were to place the scene outside the house? They are in the back yard, the front yard. They are at the mailbox, perhaps in the car. Maybe the car is moving. Who is driving? Husband or Wife?

Simply changing the physical environment of the scene *will* change the scene. It is inevitable and unavoidable.

Yes, this is a trick. Make the scene work the way you want it to work by simply changing the location, the environment.

Example #2:
Imagine a scene between two young potential Lovers. They work in the same bland and sterile office only a few desks apart. They see each other every day. The scene is set at the end of the workday. Most of the other workers have left. The Young Man decides this is his moment to make his feelings known. The scene, as written, takes place in the empty office area — rows of desks, not even cubicles — and just the Young Man and the Young Woman are there.

In the scene (as written), he suddenly starts talking to her about work. She is silent, smiling to herself, knows that he likes her (she has always felt it), and now she is waiting for him to get to the point, get specific. He struggles, can't find the courage.

So she has to help him out, guide him a bit by bringing up subjects not related to work, but something more personal. He starts to get the idea, follows suit but goes way overboard and is now moving too fast for her. Now she is wishing she never helped him, so she goes silent.

Of course he misinterprets her silence and thinks he has said something to offend her, so he backs off. Once again she has to rescue him, but does it by asking him to help her look for her pen that she pretends she has lost. This will at least bring them physically closer. He is convinced that she has lost her pen and gives the search his full effort.

When they are really close the Young Woman suddenly realizes that he is wearing an aftershave to which she is allergic. The sneezing starts immediately, but the Young Man, undaunted, continues his search for the lost pen. She drops the pen on the floor so that he can find it, and when he rises from the floor with the found pen, the Young Woman is waiting, only inches from him, ready for a kiss — but there is the problem of the runny nose.

That's the scene as written.

Okay, it's a cute scene and it all takes place in the office. But how is the environment helping us tap into the true emotions and feelings of this scene? Actually, it's not. It's just a big empty office area, no obstacles, no physical barriers to speak of.

So let's look at moving the scene.

We can start in the office. Everyone has left, leaving only the Young Man and the Young Woman. He starts talking to her; talking about work. Just when he is about to get the courage to say something personal, a Cleaning Lady comes through, emptying the wastebaskets. The Young Man's thin layer of courage disappears. He starts to walk to the door.

The Young Woman, feeling the opportunity is disappearing, runs after him, and in the hallway she changes the subject to the fact that she is having trouble sleeping lately. They are moving down the hallway when the Young Man takes the bait and starts talking about his own sleeping habits and how he has to get up in the middle of the night many times, always has and… she goes silent.

They are now standing in the lobby near the elevators. She hits a button quickly, too quickly. The Young Man is certain he has said something wrong. He goes quiet and stares at the elevator buttons. Silence. She is desperate. The elevator arrives and they both get on. Elevator going down. Time running out. The Young Woman suddenly starts searching in her purse and then has a small panic because she can't find her favorite pen. She was sure it was here. She spills her entire purse on the floor of the elevator (slipping the pen into her pocket) and the Young Man begins going through the numerous objects looking for her pen. The elevator is still moving down. Time is running out. She gets a whiff of his aftershave and has an allergic reaction, sneezing violently.

The elevator doors open and an Elderly Woman gets on. The Young Man and Young Woman are still on the floor searching. The Elderly Woman watches with bemusement. The elevator doors close and it continues the journey down. The Young Woman, desperate, drops the pen on the floor. The Elderly Woman sees this happen and thinks the Young Woman is quite clever. The Young Man finds the pen, rises to be inches away from the Young Woman's waiting lips. He sees the running nose. The elevator doors open and the Elderly Woman slips the Young Woman a handkerchief as she leaves. The doors close.

Okay, so what have we accomplished?

The Young Man leaves the office and heads to the hallway. This is a major move. Not only from one location (office) to another (hallway), but it signals that one character (the Young Man) is assuming the scene is over. Now the Young Woman is under pressure and we have started a ticking clock. How long before he is out of the office and out of the building?

They move down the hallway. Now it is a scene in motion, headed toward a destination that one seems to desire and the other doesn't. This is creating conflict within the scene while revealing the intentions of the two characters. The Young Woman starts a personal conversation in a very public place (the hallway). The Young Man now starts to reveal his own personal stories about not being able to sleep, which are a bit too much information for the Young Woman. She goes silent as they arrive in the elevator lobby. Now maybe they both want to leave. She hits the button too quickly and he goes silent.

Now we have these two conflicted individuals in the middle of actions and activities that they both desire and dread… and the clock is ticking. They get on the elevator.

They are now in a totally new environment, one that is moving them. And one that is confining them. Truly boxing them in. And they are alone, no escape. The only escape the Young Woman has is her purse and her fixation on her pen. For the Young Man the contents of the purse on the floor are an invitation, which he accepts. She smells his after-shave, which she likes (a positive reaction), but has an allergic reaction (a negative). The sneezes may push him away.

They are in a very confined and suddenly intimate environment when the door opens and an Elderly Woman gets on. She sees them on the floor, sneezing, contents of the purse on floor. She is amused (the Elderly Woman is a device. Not only does she change the environment from private to public, but she also presents an objective point of view… perhaps the audience's point of view). Suddenly, for the Young Man and Young Woman, their private environment becomes very public. The elevator doors close and it continues to move. All three are trapped. We have the conflicting relationships: two characters who desire to be together but are uncomfortable with those desires. And a third character who simultaneously becomes an obstacle and an ally, giving the couple a reason to avoid or resist their desires. The Young Woman, in desperation and perhaps embarrassment, drops the pen she was looking for. The Young Man finds it. The Elderly Woman is impressed with the manipulation. The Young Man, having found the pen, now has a logical reason to move closer to the Young Woman, despite the presence of the Elderly Woman. But it is the sight of the runny nose that causes him to pause (obstacle). Elevator doors open, Elderly Woman comes to the rescue with a handkerchief, leaves. Doors close, leaving our couple isolated and alone again, free to pursue their desires if they dare.

This above example is simple in its design. The trick here is creating obstacles and opportunities simply by changing the environment.

TRICK: ADDING AND SUBTRACTING CHARACTERS

This is a very powerful directing tool and trick. You must always keep in your mind these questions: "What would happen if someone came in to this scene?" or "What would happen if someone in the scene suddenly left?"

In the Lovers scene above we brought in two characters that are not written in the scene for the very purpose of altering the environment.

The Cleaning Lady comes through at an auspicious moment, just when the Young Man is about to find the courage to talk to the Young Woman. This intrusion creates both a relief for the Young Man (now he has good reason to abandon his objectives) and additional tension as the attempted scene suddenly becomes public. And, depending on what we have the Cleaning Lady do (clean the top of the desks of either the Young Man or Young Woman, position herself between the two, creating a barrier, turn on a vacuum cleaner, creating a noise barrier, etc.), this intrusion will totally alter the scene.

The Elderly Woman is a similar entrance but the environment is different (now it is an enclosed, somewhat private space) and she is sharing the space with the two Lovers. The Cleaning Lady has an independent activity (cleaning), while the Elderly Woman is simply present in the elevator, her objective being to ride to the first floor.

Obviously the timing of these entrances and exits is crucial. What is interrupted, what is seen or overheard... all very important. And what happens right after they leave, also crucially important. And it is in the moment after the departure of either the Cleaning Lady or the Elderly Woman that we get to witness the effect these interruptions have had on the Lovers.

TRICKS: USING OBJECTS AND PROPS

Props are potentially powerful. And they can have as much or as little power as you want to give them. In the scene above we have a few props: her purse, the pen, the handkerchief... and there could be more.

The power of the prop depends on two basic elements.

One: Is the item essential to the scene? By this we mean that the scene could not take place without this prop.

Two: If the item is not essential to the scene, how is it being used to change or alter the scene? In this scene only the pen is essential and the rest are used by the characters to express what they are feeling. All props can become very powerful depending on how they are used.

The Purse

Of course it is assumed that the Young Woman would have a purse, so at first this item has no relevance or power. But once it becomes an object or area of focus (a place to escape), it begins to take on significance. Now even the size or design of the purse becomes important. The purse becomes a third character in the scene.

Also, the contents of the purse (spilled on the floor) become additional props, either collectively or individually. It's possible that there is one item, perhaps a photograph or a prescription or an intimate personal object, that the Young Woman quickly snatches and puts back in the purse. That item, for that moment, took on power and allowed the Young Woman an opportunity to express her fear of intimacy or exposure.

The Pen

When we first hear about the pen, this object becomes important. But when we see the Young Woman remove the pen and hide it in her pocket, the power of the pen increases. Now the hiding of the pen is a metaphor for the Young Woman's desire to hide, and we can feel it. Also, the hiding of the pen is a private moment (shared only between the Young Woman and the audience), and consequently our relationship with the Young Woman has changed. We share a secret. We know something the Young Man does not.

When, in desperation, the Young Woman retrieves the pen and drops it on the floor (ostensibly for the Young Man to find), we are again sharing the secret, and then the pen gains even more power… waiting to be discovered. When we see that the Elderly Woman witnessed the deceit with the pen, our relationship with the Elderly Woman changes — she shares the secret with us.

And when the Young Man discovers the pen, this prop has now connected all three characters and finally given the Young Man the courage (or excuse) to approach the Young Woman, much to our relief.

The Handkerchief

With the offer of the handkerchief, the Elderly Woman finally engages the couple. Prior to that she had been only an observer. One simple action like this changes the constellation of characters, the relationships shift, and the handkerchief takes on a power and meaning perhaps deeper than any line could have achieved. And then, the fact that the Elderly Woman leaves the elevator and leaves the handkerchief behind means that, in some subtle way, she remains in the scene.

TRICK: EYE CONTACT

When to make it. When to break it.

By instinct actors will want to make eye contact — frequently, and often consistently. But one way of altering a performance is for you, the director, to control the moments of eye contact.

Try this. Take a simple one- or two-page scene with two characters. At first just ask the two actors to read the scene. Watch them. See the level and frequency of eye contact. Of course, if they have to read the scene off the page, they will be breaking eye contact frequently in order to find the next line. But most likely for the rest of the time they will be seeking eye contact.

Now read the scene again. This time tell the actors that they can look at each other only on the last word of each sentence they are speaking. Then they have to look away again. And when they are not speaking, they are free to make eye contact or not at any time. Now this idea of eye contact on the last word of the spoken line is obviously arbitrary. But just watch the scene.

POC: What you are looking for is the shifts and changes in attitude or emotions from both of the actors. It will happen, guaranteed. What you will witness is the power of this micro-staging.

Now it is time to move into the world of production, where every choice, every decision, every trick becomes crucial.

EXERCISES:

1. Select specific scenes from your script that you want to put into rehearsal.

2. Invite actors (could be the same ones that you used in the casting process) to join you in a rehearsal process.

3. Remember, you can be very open about what you are doing. You don't have to keep the tricks a secret. As in the casting process, you can even read the trick together and try it.

4. With these exercises, plan to spend a lot of time. Not just an hour or two on one day. Perhaps several days. Maybe meet once a week, and each time you meet you'll try a new trick or two. Give yourself time to experiment and explore.

5. Suggested tricks to try: Pause and Clip, Breaking the Continuum, Altering Seat, or Space Relationships.

6. Subtext exercises. Try them one at a time. Don't rush. They take patience.

7. Staging exercises: Be willing to experiment and explore.

8. And remember, always talk to your actors after each experiment and allow them the opportunity to express what they have experienced.

The Alchemist and The Actors in Production

So far we have used tricks in writing, casting, and rehearsal. But now is when the tricks you will use really pay off, because you are heading into the final phase — the recording of performances. All the tricks and techniques you have been using so far are merely the preparation for this final stage. It was an essential and effective preparation, but so far you have nothing from which you can make your film.

Phases of Production

There are three basic phases of the production process (in terms of performance) that must be recognized and addressed appropriately. They are:

- Rehearsal for the crew
- Rehearsal for the actors
- Shooting the scene

Each phase is an important and essential step in the process, and with each step you need to be clear about priorities and expectations.

Rehearsal for the Crew

Like a good alchemist or magician, you know when it is time to bring out the sleight of hand. You know what tricks will work at specific times. You know when they are necessary and when they are not.

You're on the set, the actors are there, ready to rehearse. The crew is there, ready to see what they are going to shoot. Everyone is waiting for you. No matter where you are, you are center stage. Time to pull out a few tricks, a little sleight-of-hand? Absolutely not. On a production day there are moments of magic, true magic, but these happen only about 10% of the time. The rest of the time is all preparation. Your job is to save your magic (and the magic of the actors) until the prime moment, when it really counts, when the cameras are rolling.

What does this mean? This means you will be showing everyone on the crew what they will be shooting. But remember: even though they need to see the entire scene, with all its staging, movement, and even rhythm and pacing… they do not need to see a performance. This is not the time for the actors to show what they can or will do. This is a time to focus on the mechanics of the scene, the staging, the coverage, and the technical challenges.

TRICK: HOLDING THE REINS

Your job is to hold the horses (the actors) back. Don't let them perform. Don't let them stretch out. Not yet. Now it is time to focus on all that left-brain stuff: the lines, blocking, staging, camera moves, lighting, sound boom placement, etc. Your job is to get this all done as efficiently and effectively as possible, so that the rest of the crew can prepare for the shoot. Once they have seen the scene, once they know what they have to do to prepare for the first shot (and subsequent shots), then it's time to pull the actors off the set and let the crew get to work.

Two basic concepts for the days of production:
1. A happy crew is a working crew… and…
2. No one waits for the director.

So a part of your job is to manage your time and your priorities so that the crew can be working while you are working… and you are working while the crew is working… and *no one* ever waits for you. With this in mind, get the actors off the set as quickly as you can so the crew can begin their work. And now it is time for you to begin working with the actors.

Rehearsal with Actors

The clock is ticking. There is a definable amount of time between this moment and the moment when the cameras start rolling. Now is the time when you, master magician that you are, have to perform some of your best magic… all in preparation for the big event (the shooting of the scene).

First, let's look at the typical sequence of events, from the rehearsal for crew until the moment when the crew is ready for you to return. Following that we will look at that small but extremely important window of time from crew ready to rolling camera.

From Crew Rehearsal to Crew Ready

As you know, this could be anywhere from ten minutes to an hour or more. Regardless, your job is the same: When the crew is ready, you must deliver the actors to the set prepared to do the scene. This means you need to make use of this time for your own preparation. Don't make the mistake that so many directors make. Don't listen to that voice in your head that says: "These are good actors, we've rehearsed the scene before, they all seem fine and focused. I am sure they will be fine."

The Actor in Production

We discussed earlier how the actor in the casting process is a totally different human being than the actor in the rehearsal process. Well, the same is true of the actor in the production process. In the casting process the actor is someone looking for a job, trying to impress the director and producers. In the rehearsal process the actor is an artist working with fellow artists and a director, focusing on developing a character, comprehending the scene, the story, and the relationships. All of this in preparation for the production process. And in the production process this actor has now transformed once again. Now the actor is a highly focused, deeply intent artist ready to deliver at the key moment. And this focus, this laser-like concentration, may also be covering up fears, concerns, apprehensions, and insecurities. It's hard to tell. Don't try to second-guess what is going on, and certainly don't make the mistake of assuming all is fine. Your job is clear. You need to deliver the actors to the set in a few minutes (or several minutes), ready to perform the scene. This means rehearsal. This means getting the actors out of their own heads and into the heads of the characters. Don't think about delivering the *actors* to the set. Think about delivering the *characters* to the set.

Make-up Room Rehearsal

When actors are in the make-up area, they are available and comfortable. This is a perfect time to begin the process of moving them from the world of the actor to the world of the character. Most actors won't want to rehearse in this environment (because it feels inappropriate), but, curiously, the character is very accessible. Start talking to the character about almost anything. And eventually bring the subject matter close to something that is contained within the scene.

This way the actor is not rehearsing the scene, but rather moving into the character, feeling the character's energy and point of view.

For example, let's imagine that we are about to shoot a scene between a Mother and her teenage Daughter. The scene is an argument. It is two in the morning and the Daughter has just come home from "visiting friends" three hours later than promised. The Mother has spent the past two hours calling the Daughter (no answer), neighbors, other parents, and even the police. You get the picture.

The two actors are sitting in their make-up chairs, side-by-side, and your job is to prepare them for the scene that they are about to do. You have two choices:

1. You can rehearse or discuss the scene, reminding the *actors* of what you want (the results you want) from the scene. Or:

2. You can prepare the *characters* for the confrontation they are about to have.

Choose the second option.

TRICK: CHARACTER PREPARATION

Get the actors' minds off the scene and plunge them into the thinking process of the characters. You do not want to send two actors in a scene with a plan of how to play the scene. But you DO want to send two characters into the scene prepared to confront each other over whatever issues might arise.

Here's how this conversation with the characters (in the make-up room) might go:

YOU
(to Mother)
It's two a.m. You've called the parents of her friend, where she was staying?

MOM
Yes.

YOU
What did they say?

MOM
She's not there. Their daughter went to sleep hours ago.

YOU
When did you call?

MOM
About half an hour ago!

YOU
Why did you wait so long? She was supposed to be home at eleven. Why didn't you call at eleven?

MOM
I don't want to be a paranoid, pushy Mom.

YOU
Like your Mom.

MOM
Exactly.

YOU
So you waited, trusted, gave her a little leeway, right?

MOM

Right.

YOU

Isn't two hours a bit of a big leeway?

MOM

Well, I....

YOU
(to Daughter, interrupting Mom)
Why didn't you call and simply say you would be late?

DAUGHTER

I did call, but nobody answered.

YOU

Did you leave a message?

DAUGHTER

I hate leaving messages. No one pays any attention to my messages.

YOU

I see. And I guess that's why you didn't answer the phone when your Mom called.

DAUGHTER

I couldn't hear it.

YOU

I see. So how the hell are you going to explain to your Mother that you weren't at Sara's house... at all? She knows, you know. You know she must have called Sara's parents. Or are you just hoping that she didn't?

DAUGHTER

Look, I got good reasons for....

YOU

You better. It's two a.m. and for all you know your mother has called the police thinking you've been kidnapped or something. You better have a really good excuse.

This interrogation can go on for a long time. But you have to be clear about something. We are not talking about the scene that these two actresses are about to do. We are simply preparing the characters for a confrontation that they are about to have. The characters don't know that there is a scene (with written dialogue). All they know is that there is a confrontation that is about to happen and they (the characters) need to get themselves ready. That's it.

Remember, your job is to deliver the actor to the set ready to do the scene and what better way than in the mindset and attitude of the character?

TRICK: THE WALK TO THE SET

The First AD has told you "we're ready." Time to bring the actors to the set. If you have been talking to the characters, you are in great shape and the actors are primed. And the "Walk to the Set" goes something like this:

Gather the actors that are in the scene. Get each character focused on a topic that relates to the content of the scene, something about which they feel passionate. Have each character start talking about that subject, not in dialogue, but in individual monologues. This is overlapping, simultaneous monologues, every character talking, only occasionally responding to each other. And once they have started, they must follow you to the set. When you arrive at the set, move them into the environment, keep them close, keep them talking. Let them continue for a couple of moments and then stop them, and thank them. Now you have delivered the actors (as the characters) to the set.

Final Rehearsal

In this final rehearsal you must allow the actors to go through the mechanics of the scene and let the crew (camera, sound, etc.) check everything for the first take. But at this point you will notice that the performance level has been elevated enormously by the Make-up Room Rehearsal and the Walk to the Set. Once the crew is ready to shoot… so are you.

POC for Shooting

Now we are at the most crucial and critical moment of the production process. And again, you must be clear about your priorities.

First, you don't need the scene to play through perfectly (whatever that means) at any time. What you do need is to capture (on film or tape) those performances out of which you will mold and shape (in postproduction) the scene. And you will need a variety of performances from which to select (bracketing).

Adjustments

The adjustments, changes, or variety in performances are either a result of the actor making new choices on how to play the scene, or a change in the emotional state and attitude of the character as he/she enters the scene. So, in order to create the variety of performances you desire, you need to stimulate adjustments either within the actor, or in the character, or both.

Result Directing

I am assuming you have a pretty clear idea of the performances you want in the scene. Most directors do, or think they do. So the question is: How are you going to ensure that you get these performances?

One way: You could just tell the actors what you want. You could be very clear about the emotional shifts and changes you feel the characters need to go through. This is Result Directing: "Here is the result I want." I am also going to assume that you know that most actors don't respond well to Result Directing because they feel their work is placed in a box, too tightly defined, no room for instinct or intuition. And they are right. So what is a director to do?

You must stop focusing on the performance. Focus on the character's needs, desires, objectives, intentions, and expectations. Talk to the characters (just like you were in the make-up room). Allow the actors to shift to the world of the character as much as possible, let them live inside that world. And by adjusting the inner life of the character, you can effectively adjust the performance in the scene without asking for a specific result.

With this concept in mind, here are the tricks you can use in the shooting process.

TRICK: THE LAST CONVERSATION

Whatever conversation the characters are engaged in just prior to the cameras rolling (and you calling 'action') will significantly affect the performances. Think about the results you want, think about what attitude or emotional state in the character may trigger those results. Have the characters engage in a conversation that will explore those attitudes and trigger those emotions, and then send them into the scene.

You may wonder how this is a trick. It is all very conscious and everyone knows what you are doing. The trick part is that you are bypassing the actor's intentions and focusing on the character's. This will allow the actor to live within the character, experience all the instincts and intuitions of the character, and it will most likely produce, organically, the results you desire. Try it. You will be amazed.

And now, with this same concept in mind, here are some more tricks:

TRICK: PEP TALK

This last conversation before "action" could also be to the self and not the other character. In other words, allow the character to talk to herself, out loud, and tell herself what she (the character) is planning on doing in the scene that is about to happen. She can 'pep' herself up, give herself courage, remind herself of her objectives, etc. And the manner, tone, and content of this 'Pep Talk' will dramatically affect her performance in the scene.

TRICK: NEW OBJECTIVE

Another simple but effective adjustment is through the character's objective, goal, or intention. Now we have to make it clear that we are talking about the *character's* objectives and not the actor's. The character is entering the scene naïve, innocent, without knowledge of the upcoming obstacles or the outcome of the scene. By simply shifting the operative verb of the objective (e.g., to seduce, to convince, to overcome, to punish, to reprimand, etc.) within the character's thinking, you will effectively alter the scene. You can make an alteration in one character's objective, or two or three, or all characters. The more alterations in the characters' objectives, the greater the change in the scene.

Again, getting back to the results you desire, you need to have a pretty clear idea of which objectives will most likely produce the results you want. And, truthfully, it is not quite that simple. It is a matter of you considering which objectives, up against specific obstacles, mixed with specific attitudes, agendas, and risks, will produce the results that you want. Now you are truly working as an alchemist. This is the magic of directing.

Stakes and Risks

Every character is risking something (has something at stake) as he/she pursues a personal objective. The greater the risk, the more dangerous the pursuit. Often these risks are unspoken, unrealized, or even unconscious. But they exist, and they greatly influence the attitude and behavior of the character.

If you want to adjust the intensity of an actor's performance, adjust the risk.

Here is an example (from JUST A RUMOR again):

Sam and Elizabeth are husband and wife, married for more than thirty years, no children. Sam had an affair with a young woman fifteen years ago. The marriage survived, barely. Sam's business partner (and best friend) Walter is younger and more charismatic than Sam. Walter and Harriet have been happily married for thirteen years and they have two children.

For the past year Walter and Harriet have been regularly sneaking away from work to meet privately. They have told no one about their private rendezvous. Sam has always assumed that Walter was having an affair. Elizabeth knew nothing.

Sam has just learned the truth from Walter.

INT. SAM AND ELIZABETH'S HOME — EVENING
An elegant Spanish styled home in the hills of
Beverly. Sam is agitated, pacing. ELIZABETH,

his wife of twenty years, sits patiently, listening. Elizabeth is a slightly plump, adorable
woman who is always eager to please.

                    SAM
        I'm speechless. Utterly speechless.
        No, I'm pissed. He's my best
        friend and I thought I knew
        everything about him. And now this.
        This big secret suddenly comes out
        and he acts like I should have
        known it all the time.

                    ELIZABETH
        And... were you ever going to
        tell me?

                    SAM
        I just learned about it today. What
        do you mean, was I ever going to
        tell you?

                    ELIZABETH
        No. I mean were you ever going to
        tell me that you thought Walter was
        having an affair?

                    SAM
        Are you kidding? Why would I tell
        you that? I tell you he's having an
        affair and then you'll want to tell
        Harriet and then I'll tell you that
        you can't and then you get worried
        that maybe I'm having another

                    SAM (CONT'D)
affair and that maybe Harriet isn't
telling you something that she
knows... And where does it all end?
No! You see, honey, my job is to be
the buddy, the pal, the best friend.
I'm the gatekeeper. I'm the one he
can talk to and who will keep his
secrets. Don't you understand that?

                    ELIZABETH
Of course I do. You cover for him
and lie for him as long as you think
he trusts you. You cover for him
even when you think he's cheating on
his wife. But when you think he's
been lying to you... and keeping
secrets from you, that's when you
come running to me for consolation.

                    SAM
I'm not coming to you for
(consolation)...

                    ELIZABETH
Of course you are. You always have,
Sam. You only want my help when
you've been wounded or betrayed. I
can count on that. But what I can't
count on is your trust in me. You've
stopped trusting me and I don't
know when that happened. And maybe
you've stopped loving me. And now I
don't know if I can trust you anymore. And I find that sad.

As we look at this scene, we need to consider the risks that each character is taking. What is truly at stake?

Sam enters the scene believing that he is going to earn Elizabeth's sympathy and maybe even her support for the violation he is experiencing. He most likely thinks the risks are low. He expects Elizabeth to get angry right along with him. The biggest risk is if Elizabeth does not understand or will not support him. And he could live with that.

Of course he is totally unaware that he is revealing a deep flaw in his character: His loyalty to Walter supersedes his trust in his wife. And even if you told him about this flaw prior to the scene, he would most likely deny it. So in order to raise the stakes for Sam, you would need to remind him of how loyal Elizabeth is to Harriet, and how she might even protect Walter. Tell him, "You need her support. If she doesn't support you, who have you got?"

Elizabeth, being the recipient in the scene, operates from a vantage point of not knowing where Sam is going or what he wants. This puts her at both a disadvantage and an advantage (this happens frequently in multi-layered scenes). She is at a disadvantage because Sam is driving the scene and she needs to ascertain where he is going and what he wants. And, for the same reason, she is at an advantage because she doesn't have to play her cards until Sam has revealed himself.

So, how do you raise the stakes for Elizabeth? Good question. And there is a simple and direct solution. Look at the scene. Look at what Elizabeth eventually does in the scene. It's clear that she takes this opportunity to finally speak her truth to Sam. She may have said these things before, maybe not recently, maybe years ago. But now that Sam is riled and vulnerable, Elizabeth shoots some well aimed daggers at his sore spots. And once you know the behavior of a character in a scene, you can 'front load' the scene by increasing the desire and risk for that behavior. For instance, you could say to Elizabeth before the scene: "When's the last time you talked to Sam about his arrogance (that you find so annoying)? Remember how arrogant and disconnected he was when he was having that affair? But he's not having another affair now, is he? Are you sure?" And even if she is just listening and not responding, you can go on: "Do you think he'll ever realize how pathetic he is, depending so much on Walter's loyalty? When's the last time he asked you for advice?" Just let her absorb these thoughts and then hit her with: "And when's the last time you really told him how you feel about him? How you see him? What you think of him? When are you going to get a little courage, Elizabeth? When are you going to stop closing your eyes?"

Now the stakes are up. The risks are great. And now you will have a scene.

Here's a suggestion for you, Dear Reader. Print out the scene above. Invite two actors to your home. Have them read the scene. Give them just enough background so that they understand the characters. And then speak to each character individually, privately, just as suggested above. Then let them read the scene again. And observe the difference.

Changes of Rhythm

We discussed Pause and Clip in Chapter Three. Quite clearly the pausing and clipping forces changes in rhythm within the scene and keeps both characters a bit off balance, which is good.

Pause and Clip are mechanical devices superimposed on a scene. There are other ways to alter the rhythms of a scene from within the character:

TRICK: CONSIDERATION

This is a very simple internal device that is guaranteed to change the rhythm of the scene. And it is character-driven, not actor-driven. Simply say to the actor/character before the scene: "There is something she (your scene partner) is going to say that won't make any sense. Find it." Now, all that this will do is refocus the character's concentration to considering every line before responding and looking for a lack of logic (and, regardless of the scene, the line or lines lacking logic will be found. Logic is very subjective). And in this consideration of the logic of each statement, the rhythm of the scene will be altered, and what the scene partner and audience will feel is the sharpened concentration of the character.

TRICK: REPETITION

This is similar to Consideration, except that this time the character is not looking for lack of logic, but rather re-framing each line. The direction before the scene: "In your mind, repeat each line she (your scene partner) says before you respond." Obviously this will cause a Pause, but what is happening during the Pause is very organic to the character. It is a natural tendency when repeating a line in your mind to separate the line from the attitude or the tone with which it was delivered. They will still both be present, but separated. This separation will impact the character's unconscious and thereby affect the delivery of the next line.

TRICK: ONE WORD

And a final technique. This time the character is not looking for lack of logic, or reframing a speech, but rather grabbing one significant word. The direction before the scene: "In each speech, find the word that you want to respond to and respond to that word." Again, the character's focus is on the text he his hearing, on the speech, and again he is looking for something within the text. This time it is one word. He may feel compelled to respond to the word as soon as he hears it, not waiting for his scene partner to finish (Clipping). Or he may find himself waiting to respond long after the speech is completed, perhaps still considering which word to choose (Pausing). Or he may respond as soon as his scene partner has finished. Either way, the rhythms of the scene are going to be affected, and all from within the character.

TRICK: OFF-CAMERA ACTOR — THE SUBTEXT BLAST

One of the unique aspects of film directing is the over-the-shoulder, single, or close-up shot, wherein one actor has his back to the camera, or is off-camera, while we see fully the performance of the actor they're interacting with. When the camera is focused on one actor in this way, we are free to allow the off-camera actor to stretch beyond and beneath the text in order to stimulate the on-camera actor. This is a very powerful and subtle technique that is used frequently in filmmaking (but of course, we in the audience never see it or hear it).

Here is how it works:

Imagine that we are shooting the scene above between Sam and Elizabeth. Sam is on-camera and Elizabeth is either off-camera, or we are shooting over her shoulder (unable to see her face or mouth). And, most likely, we have been shooting this scene for hours, spending most of the time on lighting and camera concerns and, of course, doing multiple takes of each setup. Point being, the actors have already done this scene over and over and there is a good chance that the freshness, authenticity, and immediacy of the confrontation is wearing thin.

Note: This technique that I am about to explain to you should not be tried for the first time in production. Best to introduce the actors to this technique during the rehearsal process, when the risks are very low.

Simply put, the two actors have very different responsibilities and areas of focus.

On-camera: The actor on-camera (Sam) has to say the lines as written. He cannot respond before he hears his cue line, and he has to be willing to listen to whatever the actress (Elizabeth) says to him.

Off-camera: The off-camera actress (Elizabeth) has a different job, a different focus. Her job is to be the best scene partner imaginable. Her job is to stimulate, provoke, cajole, support, defend, or attack. Whatever is going on inside her character is allowed.

The off-camera actress (Elizabeth) is allowed and encouraged to hit her scene partner with as much subtext as she wishes, accurately and honestly. The on-camera actor simply has to listen and respond with the text as written.

The above scene might go something like this. Remember, Elizabeth is off-camera and one of her jobs is to eventually give her scene partner (Sam) her lines, so that he knows when he can respond.

The added lines (subtext) are in bold.

```
                SAM
     I'm speechless. Utterly speechless.
     No, I'm pissed. He's my best friend
     and I thought I knew everything
     about him. And now this. This big
     secret suddenly comes out and he
     acts like I should have known it
     all the time.
```

                    ELIZABETH
**I really don't want to be here. I
don't want to be here at all. Please
leave me out of this.** And... were you
ever going to tell me?

                    SAM
I just learned about it today.
What do you mean, was I ever going
to tell you?

                    ELIZABETH
**Hate it. Hate it when you do that.
Reprimanding me! Criticizing me when
I ask you a simple question.** No. I
mean were you ever going to tell me
that you thought Walter was having
an affair?

                    SAM
Are you kidding? Why would I tell
you that? I tell you he's having an
affair and then you'll want to tell
Harriet and then I'll tell you that
you can't and then you get worried
that maybe I'm having another affair
and that maybe Harriet isn't telling
you something that she knows... And
where does it all end? No! You see,
honey, my job is to be the buddy,
the pal, the best friend. I'm the
gatekeeper. I'm the one he can talk
to and who will keep his secrets.
Don't you understand that?

Elizabeth takes a long pause, letting Sam's last line just hang in the air. She gives him a look as if she is about to say something, then doesn't. Finally she speaks.

> ELIZABETH
> Of course I do. You cover for him and lie for him as long as you think he trusts you. **And he doesn't trust you and you know that.** You cover for him even when you think he's cheating on his wife. **Like he did for you.** But when you think he's been lying to you... and keeping secrets from you, that's when you come running to me for consolation.

> SAM
> I'm not coming to you for (consolation)...

Elizabeth interrupts but not with words... with a movement, she turns and begins to walk away. And just as suddenly whips around and walks back next to camera and hits him with...

> ELIZABETH
> **Stop denying it!** Of course you are. You always have, Sam. You only want my help when you've been wounded or betrayed. **Like now. You poor wounded little boy. Has Daddy Walter hurt your feelings?** I can count on that. But what I can't count on is your trust in me.

```
              ELIZABETH (CONT'D)
```
**(she goes silent, letting the last
line hang in the air. Then with a
change of tone.)**

You've stopped trusting me and I
don't know when that happened. And
maybe you've stopped loving me. **Do
you have any idea how long I've
wanted to say this to you? Do you
know how frightened I am right now?
Frightened that I'll regret saying
all of this? Frightened that you
haven't heard any of this? Do you
have any idea?** And now I don't know
if I can trust you anymore. And I
find that sad.

Now I have to ask you to imagine what happened to the actor playing Sam in the scene above.

Just remember the things he was hit with during this take:

1. First he hears that his wife (Elizabeth) doesn't even want to be with him. She doesn't want to hear what he is saying. And remember that his primary objective is to get her support and sympathy.

2. Second, he is accused of reprimanding her when he was only clarifying a situation.

3. Then, after a long, detailed, and well-stated explanation of why he can't tell her everything that he knows (or believes that he knows), what does he get? Silence. A long silence. He thought he would get acknowledgement or appreciation. Then, after the long silence, Elizabeth asserts that

Walter doesn't trust him and that he knows this. And then that sneaky little reminder of when Walter covered for him during his affair.

4. And then she has the gall to walk away while he's in the middle of explaining that he is not coming to her for consolation.

5. And then another attack, accusing him of living in denial, of being a hurt little boy.

6. And then she does that silent thing again. Annoying.

7. And then she says *she's* frightened of what she is saying. And frightened that Sam hasn't been listening or won't understand. More criticism! And all Sam wanted was a little support.

And all of this while he is on-camera, while he is silent. He has no words to respond to all of this. He is not allowed to defend or explain, he can only listen, and then respond when the script allows him to. And in that listening, in those silent moments, the character of Sam is obviously having feelings and thoughts, and the camera will pick it all up. All of it. This is magic. This is gold. This is what we alchemists are looking for, what we are trying to craft from all these raw materials.

It's A Wrap!

We are now mining gold. We are now "transmuting a common substance, perhaps of little value, into a substance of great value." We are accomplished alchemists!

And now it is time to hear words of wisdom from some of my favorite wizards.

EXERCISES:

1. Now that you have completed Chapter Four, it's time to rent the movie whose script you selected at the end of Chapter One and see the film you have been working on.

2. Watch the film. Especially the scenes you selected for your discussions with the 'writer,' for the casting process and for the rehearsal process.

3. Watch these scenes closely. Watch them several times.

4. In your script, write the difference between what you experienced watching the scene and your initial vision and experiences of working on these scenes.

5. Remember, they will be different. But one is not better than the other. Just different interpretations. You may like your ideas better, fine. You may like what the director of the film did better, fine. Write it all down. This is where you will learn more about the individual expression in filmmaking. And you will begin to see and feel your own voice as a filmmaker.

Words of Wisdom From Some Wonderful Wizards

As directors, we all develop our own styles of directing and how we work with writers and actors. It was always my intention in this book to include interviews with a variety of working directors in theater, film, and television. In the following interviews you will have the privilege of learning some tricks, tools, and techniques from some of Hollywood's finest directors.

Interview with
ARTHUR SEIDELMAN

Arthur Seidelman is an award-winning American television, film and theatre director and an occasional writer, producer and actor. Seidelman made his screen directorial debut with *Hercules* in New York, a 1970 comedy-action film starring Arnold Schwarzenegger. Additional credits include *The Caller, Walking Across Egypt, Puerto Vallarta Squeeze*, and *The Sisters*. Most of Seidelman's career has been spent in television, directing movies such as *Macbeth, Like Mother Like Son: The Strange Story of Sante and Kenny Kimes*, and *A Christmas Carol*; episodes of series such as *Fame, The Paper Chase, Knots Landing, Hill Street Blues, Magnum, P.I., Murder, She Wrote, Trapper John, M.D., L.A. Law*, and *A Year in the Life*, among others.

I first met Arthur Seidelman when he spoke on a panel at the DGA (Directors Guild of America). I was so impressed with his passion, insights, range of experience, and his deep determination to share that experience with other directors, that I knew I had to meet him. And I immediately knew I wanted him to be in my book. We met a few weeks later for breakfast near his office in Westwood, California. It was all that I had hoped: A passionate discussion of storytelling, directing, acting, and writing. I gave him a copy of *Directing Feature Films* and he made a commitment to be part of *The Film Director's Bag of Tricks*. For this interview we met at the famous Aroma Café in Toluca Lake, CA.

MARK TRAVIS: Arthur, I want to focus on working with writers and actors. You work in television, film, and theatre. I know there are a lot of similarities, but the differences are profound.

ARTHUR SEIDELMAN: Very different working with writers, working with actors. One of the key differences in working with actors, there are subcategories. Theatre is different from film. Film tricks/techniques are designed to get an immediacy of response, to get it right now, to get it on film. Theatre needs to implant something that is going to stay and grow so it doesn't go away after one or two performances. For example, when working with an actor in a film situation, one trick I'll use is, say you're doing a scene and there are moments in the scene the actor is not getting. You've got a scene that's a page long and you're getting 2/3 of the page but 1/3 of the page isn't happening. All you need to do is create a situation that causes the actor to get that 1/3 even if you mess up the other 2/3 because you've already got the other 2/3 (on film). So the responsibility of the director is to keep track in your inside calculator — 'okay I've got that speech and that speech, don't have this one and this one. How do I get what I want for this one and this one even if the technique I'm going to use will throw off the other ones?' Don't worry about the other ones — you've already got them. One trick you can use for those few speeches you haven't gotten yet is the old "as if": "That's great. Now why don't we try doing this as if you were speaking to a six-year-old child" or "Let's do the scene as if you had just run a mile and you're exhausted." Whatever the "as if" is, as long as it activates the speeches you have not gotten, doesn't matter if it throws off the rest. As long as you get what you need.

MT: I am constantly reminding directors that it's not important ever to get the perfect performance. It's only important that you end up with the material you need so you can create the performance you want.

AS: Provided you know how to keep track of what you have.

MT: And provided you have a clear idea in your head what will work, because you're not going to see it work that way on the set.

AS: You're constantly editing. You have to. If you're waiting for the perfect take for the whole scene, then you're over schedule.

MT: Exactly.

AS: You can use anything. I've done things like make a loud noise happen off-stage, off-camera, to get a reaction. You have to capture it moment-by-moment, beat-by-beat. It doesn't matter if it's in six different takes. As long as you have each moment.

MT: So you're doing whatever you can while shooting, whatever you feel is necessary that will trigger the reaction, the emotions, the responses, the attitudes, or whatever you need, almost moment to moment, within a scene.

AS: Yes.

MT: Knowing you will piece it together in postproduction.

AS: Times I have said to myself, "That's not the reaction I want. But I'm not going to be on him then. I'm going to be on her."

MT: Or you go back and shoot that reaction again with another stimulus from off-camera so you get a reaction of wonderment rather than shock (for instance), and in editing you'll put that reaction in response to a specific line. It's a performance the actor never gave you.

AS: You are really a manipulator. There's no better word, and you're twisting and manipulating people to get the totality, which exists only in your mind. What I've said to producers, what I've said to lots of people is, "Don't worry about that. I've seen the movie. I'm the only one who has seen the movie, and I know what the movie is, and that's what I'm getting on film. I'm getting as close as I can to the movie I've already seen."

MT: In the casting process, how concerned are you about being able to stimulate this particular actor? Are you testing to see if this actor is going to respond to these techniques you're talking about?

AS: What I look for in the casting process is emotional availability and a trained actor, an actor who has technique, not waiting for inspiration to strike him or her. I get worried when an actor comes into a reading and does a performance. They're ready for you to roll camera. Chances are that's all you're ever going to get, and that's not good. That's true of theatre or film. What I'm looking for is a basic understanding of the character, a sympathy, you know, an empathic response to the character, an emotional and intellectual availability.

MT: How are you testing that in the casting process?

AS: That is so intuitive. It's in conversation. It's an essence you get from a person. So hard to qualify or quantify it. It's very difficult.

MT: On instinct with each person?

AS: Sure. Does the actor seem to be someone who enjoys the process of collaboration? What training has the actor had? With whom have they studied? *Have* they studied? That's a big part of it for me. If I know I have an actor who spent a few years with Sandy Meisner, that's someone who's been exposed to a language, a vocabulary, a technique that I can utilize. Have they studied with Strasberg or his successors? It's a different language, but there's a language. If all they studied was with some shtick hack, or if all they've studied is at some college or university, then that's probably worthless, so that's a significant part of how I respond.

MT: I have two questions concerning your rehearsal process. One: In terms of developing the characters, the scenes, or exploring the variables you have with each actor, what works for you and what doesn't? And, secondly, how much are you telling the actors about the way you work in production? Or are you telling them anything?

AS: I do try to tell them by example, but I do let them know how it's going to be. And the essential thing (and this is true in film and in theatre), as much as possible, lead the actor to believe that every idea is their own. At the opening of the first showing of *The Sisters* at the Tribeca Film Festival, someone did a Q&A and asked a question of Maria Bello: "What happens if you come into a scene with an idea that is very different than Arthur's about how the scene should be done?" Maria gave a very honest answer. "Well, Arthur lets me try whatever my idea is and then he kind of leads us to a different interpretation which was always what he wanted but now we think we thought of it."

MT: That's great.

AS: That's the job. Because if it comes from outside it's always, no matter how gifted they are, it's always a little bit stuck on them, always a little bit external. If you can lead them to believe they thought of it, it's theirs, there's the excitement of an idea that came from inside. It's much more deeply implanted than "the director asked me to do it this way." Very important.

MT: Great. Now in terms of your ways of shooting.

AS: It's a matter of trust. I think it's important that when an actor says, "Can I try this?" you never say no. Never say no, even if you know it's not going to work, or it's the most ridiculous idea. You cannot cut off their creativity, because if you do that you're turning the fire down. You want them to have the freedom to try anything, then you pick and choose and "Oh, that was great" even if it's something like "Let me do this scene as if I've had too much wine at dinner," and you don't want that, you don't want the character to be a wine drinker. "Alright," you say, "Let's try it," because out of that experience, even if you just get through the scene that way and you say, "That really didn't work because, oh, yeah, right, I just realized she's not a wine drinker," you learn something about the character.

MT: And the line, "No, she's not a wine drinker." Is that coming from you or from her?

AS: Hopefully from her.

MT: If it comes from her then you lead her to the discovery that her idea is not going to work.

AS: And now she knows more about the character than she did before. And not being a wine drinker causes something else to happen in the character. So everything you try or the actor tries, even if the result was a rejection of the idea, has added to your knowledge of the character.

MT: Knowing what the character is *not* is part of knowing the character.

AS: Right. But the important thing is never say, "No, don't try that." You might say, "Why do you want to try that?" But never say no. You can discuss it, but if you turn them off, they're off.

MT: How about when the actor wants to do another take?

AS: In terms of requests for another take, you have to know how hungry the actor is for that other take, because they're going to go home at night whipping themselves. Give them the other take. If it's just a whim and you really don't need it, tell them why. "Oh, no, no, I got that. Believe me, trust me. I got that beautifully. Let's move on." But if it's, "No, no, I really don't like what I did," give it to them. Funny story of John Ford. One of his first films with John Wayne, it's a shot of Wayne riding in, getting off a horse. Got a great take. Wayne says, "I really wasn't graceful, need another take, really want another take." Okay, change the load on the camera. Okay, action. Wayne rides in again. Okay, cut. You like that one, Duke? That one feel better? "Yeah, yeah, that's much better." You really liked that one? "Yep." John Ford walked over to the camera, took the load (of exposed film) off. Handed it to Wayne. "It's yours." Wayne never again asked him for another take. The other famous Ford story: When he was told by the studios he was ten pages behind schedule, he said, "Can I have the script, please?" Found the ten pages, ripped them out and said, "Okay, I'm on schedule now." Your greatest asset is the actors' creativity. Their freedom. The fact is they need to trust you as a safety net and if you squelch that you're just hurting yourself. Not worth it. The things that drive you crazy are the actors who want to discuss. You have to put the brakes on so you say, "Okay, let's try it and see what happens. Let's not talk about what's going to happen. Let's experience what's going to happen."

MT: I feel that the greatest untapped resource in this town is the actors' creativity.

AS: Absolutely, absolutely.

MT: It's a crime what we do to actors most of the time. We write a script, for theatre or the screen, we raise a lot of money. Then we bring in a lot of actors and we try to fit them in these little boxes called 'characters' and we hope they're going to fit into what we've created and 90% of their creative potential is shut down.

AS: Exactly. You have to allow for them, and it's what I tell writers. You do an outline and you sit down to write your script. Allow it to change. Let it grow. Before I go to work every morning I know exactly every shot I'm going to do, and then it all changes because if you're lucky enough, you have an actor who makes something happen that you never thought of. If you just have actors who do what you've already thought of, how boring. So the movie in your mind is still going to be there. It's the same movie, but let it grow and change and happen in more vivid colors than you ever imagined it could.

MT: How do you work with difficult writers? I don't mean difficult people, but difficult situations.

AS: What you have to do is make the writer feel that you want to make his or her movie, that you're not coming to take what they've written and change it into some other thing. That your job is to fulfill their story. I'm getting inside your story. I'm not standing outside to use you for some other end. I'm going to fulfill your vision, maybe in ways you haven't imagined, but it's still your vision, your dream. That's the essential thing.

MT: So they feel you are there to serve them.

AS: Exactly. To serve them. But not to serve *them*. To serve the story. The story is more important than you or me. The story has its own identity, its own life, and you are there to fulfill it and protect it.

MT: The story is more important than the script.

AS: Absolutely. The script is a manifestation of the story.

MT: There's a million ways that script could tell the same story. My service as a director is to the story, not the script.

AS: Exactly. But you're on the same team as the writer.

MT: So you're working with a writer. You like the story, but are determined to develop a better script. How do you work with the writer?

AS: Explain why.

MT: Really?

AS: Yes. You have established the fact that you're on the same team, that you want to make his/her movie. One piece doesn't feed that as well as it could or should. Explain clearly what's missing and why having it there would be beneficial. Don't demand. Lead them to your conclusion. Favorite writer story — working with producer Renée Valente. Great lady. Started as a casting director, became one of the first really successful lady producers in features and TV. Working with a writer on a film starring Elizabeth Taylor on location in Arizona, doing rewrites on a scene. Brought it in to us, put it in front of us. Renée read the scene and said, "You're such a gifted writer, a wonderfully talented, gifted writer, that I know you can do better than this." Gotta be on the same team. Can't make the writer feel you're using them. Respect where it started. Respect who was there when the page was blank. It's essential to communicate with a writer. They're not for hire. They're not hacks. Have to go in and say, "Okay, I'm going to tell you what I think the problem is. I don't know how to solve it. You know how to solve it."

MT: Giving credit for the solution even before he's heard the problem.

AS: Exactly. My job is to say, "This scene should end with a punch in the stomach and I'm getting a slap on the shoulder.

Help me." I got the easy job. I get to say, "This isn't quite working. You have the tough job. You have to figure out how to make it work."

MT: Right. Now, if the writer is totally disagreeing with you....

AS: Then there does come a time when the writer may have been on the project too long, too close. Sometimes you need to bring in another writer. Same as editing. If I insist on every cut the way I thought of it, and the editor is saying no, then maybe I'm too close to it. Need another pair of eyes that are fresh. If a writer is not open to that, then maybe you need to bring in another pair of eyes. Again, your responsibility is to the movie or play. No one can stand in the way, not even the one who thought of it in the first place.

MT: And what if an actor starts fighting you.

AS: If it's in the middle of production, then anything you need to do to get the performance you want. If they're angry at you, use the anger. If you need to insult them, insult them. We're manipulators. We're sons of bitches. We'll do anything we need to in order to get that moment on film.

MT: Have you ever regretted anything you've done?

AS: No. Unless it was not doing enough to get what I needed. If it got me what I wanted, then no. The film will live on. Not my relationship with an actor. Who cares? It's what I got on film. People aren't seeing whether or not that actor and I are bosom buddies. They are seeing that movie.

MT: Do you ever direct an actor through another actor?

AS: Oh sure. Let's say I'm on her (the actress) now. I know when I did your side (the other actor), you were tough with her. I need (you) to melt her a little bit. Make love to her with your eyes, your voice. Let me see how she reacts to that.

MT: Using the off-camera actor to try to stimulate something different. Again, this is going back to your saying, "I know how this is going to cut together later."

AS: Oh, yeah. I need that moment. I want that look. Stick your tongue out at her. Grab his cock.

MT: I've had actors off-camera do subtext rather than text. Just throw subtext at her. Force her to listen to this barrage of raw feelings and emotions.

AS: Oh, yeah. She's used to your doing that line that way. Throw her a curve. Let me see what happens.

MT: These are all getting back to the manipulation. So interesting. We're storytellers, we're manipulators. So many people are offended when I use that term, 'manipulation.' They think it's a negative. But every storyteller is a manipulator. We go to see a film or a play because we want to be manipulated.

AS: Absolutely. Affect me.

MT: Beat me up, if you want.

AS: Absolutely. Get to me.

MT: Trick me, even.

AS: Absolutely. What did Hitchcock do except fuck with your mind?

MT: Brilliantly.

AS: And you love it.

MT: And you go home and you're thrilled because you've been messed up.

AS: When I go home and I'm not thrilled is when nothing got to me. I want to be fucked with, manipulated, affected. Don't want to be left untouched. That's boring.

MT: So, what do you think is the most important training for filmmakers?

AS: Watch movies. Classic movies. Billy Wilder, Ford, all the giants. Orson Welles said the three most influential directors were John Ford, John Ford, and John Ford. Watch not just what was done yesterday. Learn the basics of your trade. Read, read, read. And work with actors. Don't just learn about lenses. You have two friends who are actors? Get them in your living room, give them *The Glass Menagerie,* and get from them the performances you want. Find out how to do that. What did you have to say to her to get her to do that the way you envisioned her doing that? How did you get her to not get it? Work with actors. They are the colors on your palette, and if you don't know what to say to them, you're not going to paint your painting. So watch movies, read, work with actors. Learn all the technical stuff. That's easy. If you don't know it, hire a DP who does know it. That's the easy part. It's learning storytelling that's tough.

Interview with
GORDON HUNT

Gordon Hunt has been nominated twice by the Directors Guild of America for the Best Director of a Television
Comedy. He won the award for the "Alan Brady Show"
episode of *Mad About You*. Gordon was the director of fifty
episodes and pilots, including *Frasier, Caroline in the City,
Suddenly Susan*, and many others. He directed episodes that
won Emmy Awards for both Mel Brooks and Carl Reiner.
Gordon has directed some of our finest actors, including:
Jeremy Irons, Kristin Chenoweth, Anthony Edwards, Felic-
ity Huffman, Brian Stokes Mitchell, Helen Hunt, BJ Ward,
Anne Heche, Alan Arkin, Ed Asner, James Cromwell, and
Sharon Gless. Gordon Hunt was Head of Casting at the
prestigious Mark Taper Forum in Los Angeles for nine
years. He is the author of the best-selling theatre book, *How
To Audition*.

I have known of Gordon Hunt for my entire acting and directing career in Los Angeles. For nine years Gordon was the
casting director at the Mark Taper Forum (the prestigious
regional theatre in Los Angeles), and while I was working
both as an actor and a director I would occasionally get the
opportunity to audition for Gordon. Even back then I was
in awe of his talent, patience, and obvious affection for actors
and theatre. Sadly, he never cast me in any of his productions.
Then, when his daughter, Helen Hunt, rose up through the
acting ranks and became a formidable star, I felt that a lot
of this had to do with the coaching talents of her father. I
heard both Gordon and Helen speak at the DGA on a panel
discussing "Working with Actors," and knew immediately
that I wanted Gordon for this book. Here are the words and

wisdom of one of the most knowledgeable directors in Los Angeles. We met at Gordon's serene home, nestled amongst the oak trees in the Hollywood Hills.

MARK TRAVIS: Gordon, you have worked with a lot of writers in theatre and television, what tools or tricks do you use to get them to see what you possibly see, or to get them to do the rewrite that you want?

GORDON HUNT: When I was working in theatre I would work a lot with writers when we were doing a play. And I'd spend a lot of time hashing it out with writers (playwrights). And a trick that I would use would be to put the scene that I feel is not working on its feet and show the writer specifically where it feels to me like it's not happening in performance, so he has it right in front of him, and he has it fresh in his head, and he can either agree with me or disagree with me. That's in the rehearsal process. Otherwise, for me it is just going through the script by myself and putting little check marks where I feel things aren't working and a little note why. And then go through these with the writer and say, "It feels to me like there is a problem here. What do you think?" And put the ball in their court. Because, you know, unlike the movie business, the writer (playwright) is king.

MT: So when you say, "It feels like there is a problem here," do you know in your mind what you think the problem is?
GH: Oh, yeah.

MT: But you won't say it. Are you leading them to find what you think you already know?
GH: As much as I can. If I can make it their idea it's a better shot than setting up some kind of difference (of opinion) that might crop up and get worse later.

MT: Right. To me, that's a trick, or a tool. Get the writer to discover the problem that I already see. If I tell the writer there is a problem, chances are he will resist it.

GH: Absolutely possible. Because the idea didn't come from him. A lot of times I'll say, "Here's a thought. Look at this. It seems to me that there is a problem. We'll talk tomorrow." So it doesn't become a sit-down. But if he immediately says, "Oh yeah, I get it," then fine. But otherwise give him 24 to 48 hours.

MT: So it percolates.

GH: Exactly.

MT: You don't let him off the hook and you don't put the pressure on.

GH: That's right.

MT: That's very clever. Now with directing television and working with those writers.

GH: In television, you (the writer) don't have the say that you have as a writer in the theatre. The producers have the say. The producer/writers have the say. I sit in on a lot of (re-writing) sessions, but the final word is not mine.

MT: You have directed mostly four-camera sitcoms. And now you are dealing with a producer who has hired you, who is also one of the writers, and you are labeled 'the director,' and theoretically you would think that on the totem pole of power, the director is above the writer. But the writer is the producer. How do you deal with this writer/producer team?

GH: The best method I have for dealing with that is knowing the script ahead of time. And a lot of times you don't get the script until Monday at four a.m. (the day of the first reading).

You've got to read the script, make those check marks and notes, and come in armed with information. Come in with the problems, and ideally come in with suggestions, solutions. You want them to realize you are not attacking their writing, but you are trying to help.

MT: And when you hear that first reading, are some of the problems taken care of by the actors?

GH: Yes, sure.

MT: And I would also assume that there are problems that come up in the reading that you didn't anticipate.

GH: Absolutely. And sometime jokes that work in the reading that you didn't anticipate. Or jokes that don't work. It works both ways.

MT: But when you want a rewrite from the producer/writer team, do you suggest it as softly as you suggested with playwrights: "I think there could be a problem here. What do you think?" Or are you giving them more concrete solutions?

GH: I would think, especially with a sitcom, because it is such a transitory form (the writers write it and throw it out there and then they throw it back the next night in a rewrite). I would still say, "Here's the problem. Here's a possible solution. What do you think?"

MT: What about the rehearsal process? You've worked both in theatre and television. In directing sitcoms there is a significant amount of rehearsal time (two to three days) compared with other forms of television. In terms of working with actors in rehearsal, what techniques or tricks do you use to help them get to where you think they need to go or where you want them to go?

GH: Well, when I give the actors notes I try to make it one-on-one. Even if it is just a whispered word to somebody as I walk by them. So you're not announcing in front of the company that 'this guy is not good,' or 'this guy is ruining the scene.'

MT: So you keep the notes to the actors as private as possible.

GH: Yeah. I'm not sure where I got that, but I know I read one of the many biographies of Kazan (Elia Kazan), and a lot of actors would talk about how he would come up to them at the last minute and say something like, "You're thirsty." So the actor suddenly had something to latch onto. It's that kind of 'trickery.' Perhaps if it's the timing of a joke. I know I did an episode of *Suddenly Susan* and Eric Idle was on it. It's my great moment in sitcom directing. We were doing a scene and Eric had something to say. I don't remember what it was now, but I went down after the first rehearsal and I said to him, "You know, if you give us 'that much' air before the line it might work better." Meanwhile I am swallowing and gulping because who am I to tell Eric Idle how to time anything? But he did it, and it worked. So....

MT: And that is a trick (see Pause and Clip). And are there other things that you will tell an actor privately to help them?

GH: Yeah, like, "Fight for the power in the scene." Who has the power, where is the power? Or, "You're missing the joke because you're not listening." Because that's wrecking the rhythm.

MT: And do you think the actor is not listening because he is anticipating the joke?

GH: Either that or he is trying to remember his next line. Either way, you're not getting an honest reaction, a real reaction to the line. And therefore the joke is not real.

MT: Gordon, you've directed a lot of comedy. Do you think you can take an actor who is inherently not funny and make them work well within comedic material?

GH: Very rarely, if at all. I look for the amount of humor (in the actor), whether it is a serious drama or a comedy. If an actor doesn't have that sense of humor, it probably means that they don't have that timing that makes humor and they don't know how to… let go and just be free with something. People with humor seem to have that. The best example I have of that in my repertoire is Brando in *Streetcar* (Marlon Brando in *A Streetcar Named Desire*). He found tons of light moments and jokes in that material. And normally you would look at that script and say, "This is a long and serious ride." But he found funny stuff… and that is the kind of actor I look for. An actor who knows where humor sits in things. Let it have its humorous moments even though it is serious material. Humor (in serious material) will pull the audience right into the piece. If I finally find myself, as an audience member, able to let go and I'm laughing, that means I've forgotten everything for a moment and I am really part of what is going on in the room.

MT: The casting process. You were at the Mark Taper Forum for many years.

GH: For nine years.

MT: How many productions did you cast in that time?

GH: We did six to eight productions a year on the main stage. Plus we did eight to ten plays of an experimental nature, plus stage readings. And I cast some outside productions for Gower Champion and other directors. So I don't have a number for you.

MT: Hundreds.

GH: Yeah.

MT: And besides being the casting director, were you also directing at that time?

GH: Yeah, I was.

MT: So, whether you are casting for another director or for yourself, what advice do you have for us? What tricks, tools, or techniques really serve you in the casting process? And you've had the rare opportunity of observing many directors as they work with actors in the casting process.

GH: A great education.

MT: So, what advice do you have for us?

GH: First pronouncement: Casting is 90-95% of your job. Getting the right person for the part. And then, as the director, knowing what it is that you are looking for. A lot of the casting happens for me in the first two or three minutes after the actor walks through the door. It has to do with a kind of vibe they give off. Sometimes you can get a sense of insecurity that comes out with a joke of hostility hidden behind it somewhere. It's that uncomfortable position that some actors feel the audition process puts them in. The truth of the matter is that they put themselves in that. They don't have to come and audition. But if they want to, the more — talk about tricks — the more tricks they can have that are truthful tricks that allow them to be who they are, the better off they are. I try my best to put them at ease, if I can — with a little humor if I've got it that day. I ask them if they have questions, or anything they want to know before we start. And then I like to tell them not too much about what's going on in the play, because I want to see two things: One, did they do their homework? And two, I'd like to see where their instincts take them without having instructional information from me. Because what I will be working with will be their own instincts.

MT: You've seen thousands of actors audition. How many actors do you think come in with an idea of what *you* want versus a very clear idea of what they, the actor, wants?

GH: Good question. And this is something I try to teach in my acting class as well: "White is interesting. Black is interesting. Grey is not so interesting." By that I mean, the actor who tries to double-guess me, who tries to figure out what I want and doesn't make choices that are instinctive to them, is not that interesting. But the actor who makes instinctive choices shows me that there is something to work with. The actor who comes in being careful and not wanting to do something that might take the part away from him, or put him out of the running, is in the grey area. Not interesting.

MT: Do you think a lot of actors do that?

GH: Yes. It's out of fear. You can sometimes see through that and throw an idea at him to shake him out of that 'being careful' state.

MT: I would rather have them be bold and be way off, than be careful and close.

GH: Exactly. Because then you have something to play with, to work with. I tell actors, "You cannot predict or control the outcome of an audition in terms of your employment. But what you can do is remember that you love to act, and when you go into an audition it is nothing more than an opportunity to act for five minutes. And do that thing that you love. And then you go home. And if something comes of it, fine. And if it doesn't, fine."

MT: If you have an actor reading for you (and you are the director) and you feel there is potential here in terms of what you are looking for, what do you do with them in the time that is left in order to explore their range, flexibility, etc?

GH: I try to connect it to the material we are working on. At the moment I am casting for Motion Capture / Video Game. We're running the auditions just like we do for theatre. I'll give them an adjustment to see how well they can take an adjustment. Do they really listen when I have something to say?

MT: What about callbacks?

GH: I find callbacks very useful. I've seen actors come in and nail it the first time, and even so I'd like to see a callback because sometimes that first time was just a fluke and they can't get back there again. I feel more secure having seen them do it in two different time periods and two different circumstances.

MT: Maybe that fluke was all they had.

GH: Right.

MT: Or when you put them with another person and suddenly it's gone? And they have nothing else?

GH: Absolutely. There's also another thing that can happen. Sometimes there's another person in the room who wasn't there the first time. Maybe a producer. And sometimes that person will be giving off a vibe which makes the actor nervous and the actor won't know where it's coming from. I've seen that happen a lot. Just by their persona. It's strong. It's very strong.

MT: And what do you do when you see that?

GH: I try to calm them down, give them a little humor, hopefully, and a couple of words of wisdom… and ask them to do it again. But it's an interesting phenomenon. And often the more callbacks an actor gets the more nervous he gets because he's getting closer. It's not an easy thing being an actor.

MT: You've directed your daughter, Helen.

GH: Yeah, many times.

MT: How is it different than directing any other actress?

GH: It really isn't different. Because we have this relationship where we are more friends than father and daughter. But then after a couple of seasons (*Mad About You*, starring Helen Hunt and Paul Reiser) she became one of the producers. So I'm working for her along with five or six other producers. That was fun.

MT: Let's talk about production. Since you've done primarily multiple-camera sitcoms… how do you work with the actors when you are shooting a scene? Again, I am talking about the tricks. And I am going to remind you of a trick you told me about when I first asked you to do this interview. Tell you what, I'll state the problem and you tell me the trick.

GH: Okay.

MT: The problem is: You're shooting a scene and one actor continually gives a poor reading on one specific line. It's not the reading or intention or attitude that you want.

GH: Right. You do a pick-up. Immediately. Let's say the line is "I have to get *out of* here." And that's the emphasis I want.

And the actor keeps saying it emphasizing the word "have," like this: "I *have* to get out of here." But that's not what I want. So I will tell everyone we're doing a pick-up (starting with that line) and as I'm walking away from the camera I'll say, "All right everybody, we're taking it from 'I have to get *out* of here.'" And that's the reading I want him to do, without telling him how to do it.

MT: Brilliant. You're giving him a line reading without really giving him a line reading. Does it usually work?

GH: It almost always works. The actor has no idea what has happened.

MT: This is brilliant, Gordon. Not only are you getting the reading that you want, but by starting a pick-up on a specific line, a problem line, the actor is now thinking of starting this take on that line and just this fact will give the line a new energy, a new reading, an altered intention.

GH: That's true. Absolutely. You know, Mark. I just thought of something that maybe isn't a trick. I have found that when somebody is really doing their homework and has really put an effort into the work, you need to really appreciate it. Tell them something is good. Because so often they have heard, "No, no, that'll never work." Remind them. And remind yourself. Say, "Good for you. You got it. You nailed it." Just keep stroking them, because it's hard work that they are doing.

MT: This is great.

GH: And another trick, when you have a note to give them, start out with, "I really like what you did on Page 27. And when you get to Page 28, how about if you do this?" So you begin it on a positive note. As a director, I prefer the idea of being hired to help the actors, not *direct* them or *command* them. But to help them get what they brought in. That's my job.

MT: Sometimes I feel that 'director' is the wrong name for what we do. You're saying we guide and we coach, we comfort and create a safe environment where they can play and explore. There are a lot of things we do that don't sound like 'directing.'

GH: Right. And another trick. At the table reading. Get at the head of the table. That's your seat, where you should be. Start out with a welcome with some humor in it. And just, without being dictatorial, allow yourself to take over the room. So they know, if they have a question, you are the one they are going to, no one else.

MT: That's a tricky balancing job.

GH: It is.

MT: ...to be open and relaxed, and at the same time to let everyone know that you are in charge. Especially in episodic television, where there are producers around who are always in charge... but you have to be in charge that week.

GH: Exactly.

MT: I am sure you have run into this situation: The guest actor on a sitcom. The guest actor who is terrified. Good actor, talented, maybe working well in rehearsal, but as the cameras come in and the audience is about to come in for the live taping, you can feel the terror building. What do you do to help them?

GH: Boy, it depends so much on the person. You stroke them. You encourage them. There was a musical I directed and there was one guy who had a crucial scene and he couldn't get it, couldn't get it. And I had done everything I could. And I knew I had only one more chance with him. So I brought him out on dress rehearsal day into the lobby and I went through the scene line by line. I gave him line readings. I told him "louder" and "softer." And I just grabbed that sucker and just shook it out of him. And it worked. And I never had a chance to do it before or since. But it worked.

MT: It's interesting. That's result directing.
GH: Right.

MT: Sometimes that's all you have left to work with.
GH: Right.

MT: If it gives us the performance we need, that we want....
GH: That's what we are there for.

MT: And if it scares them into a performance, we'll take it.
GH: Absolutely.

MT: Our job as directors is to deliver the product. The actor has to deliver the character, which is only a small part of the product. We're responsible for the whole mess. And if he (the actor) ends up hating me in the end, too bad. As long as I got a good product.
GH: It's show business.

Interview with
MARK RYDELL

Mark Rydell is an Academy Award–nominated director, a classically trained actor, and an accomplished jazz pianist. Trained for the arts at Juilliard, Neighborhood Playhouse and the Actor's Studio, Mark Rydell was a busy actor and musician throughout the 1950s. In the early '60s, Rydell established himself as a dependable series-TV director. His first film directorial assignment was 1968's *The Fox*; 13 years later, he garnered an Oscar nomination for his direction of *On Golden Pond* (1981). In 1973, Rydell made a surprise return to acting at the request of his old friend Robert Altman, portraying a sadistic gangster boss in Altman's *The Long Goodbye*; he has since essayed supporting roles in *Punchline* (1988) and *Havana* (1989), the latter directed by another former actor, Sidney Pollack. Rydell is a Board Member of the Actors Studio and an Artistic Director of the Actors Studio West. He shares from his filmmaking experience at universities and seminars all over the country.

I first met Mark in 1980 in Rockport, Maine, where he was teaching a directing workshop. I was fortunate enough to be accepted as a student. He was in postproduction on *On Golden Pond*. I had, of course, seen many of his films: *The Fox*, *Cinderella Liberty*, *The Cowboys*, and was totally blown away by the power of *The Rose*.

We stayed connected, and several years later I had the rare opportunity of working with Mark in his production company, Concourse Productions, for two years, developing scripts and future projects for him to direct. Just spending time with Mark in the creative storytelling process is an education that can never be matched.

A few years ago, Mark invited me to join the Actors Studio and again I had another rare treat. For several months he and I ran a directors workshop within the Studio, working with some of the finest actors in Los Angeles.

The evening I interviewed Mark was just two days before the 30th Anniversary screening of *The Rose*, presented by the Academy of Motion Picture Arts and Sciences. We discussed the importance of this film, the breakthrough performance of Bette Midler, and how honored Mark was that his work was being honored by the AMPAS. Then we got down to discussing filmmaking.

MARK TRAVIS: You've worked with a lot of writers, Mark. And I've had the pleasure of watching you work with some of the best. And I remember some of your stories about working with Ernest Thompson (playwright and screenwriter of *On Golden Pond*). You said you were holed up in his hotel for days and weeks.

MARK RYDELL: He'd written this play, which was a smash, but it was a farce. It was directed and written as a farce on Broadway — a nakedly comedic execution of the play. And I said, "I know you've had great success (we'd started to write the screenplay) and you want to do it the same way, but you're making a mistake, because we have an extraordinary situation here. You have Katharine Hepburn and Henry Fonda, who are great and facing death, and that is what's rumbling under the whole picture — this concept of death and its imminence. And he's confronting it, and she keeps trying to buck him up." When they first come in the house, I designed a scene that wasn't in the script. Henry Fonda had had a long career by that point, and I had photos of him at all ages, and I put these photos on the mirror. When he walks in, he walks to the mirror and is looking at the pictures. Had a picture of him all young and muscled, and pictures of him older, which I had placed in various spots. He looked at each picture, each one got older and older, and finally it was a picture of him retiring from his job as a teacher, and he looked at these pictures one at a time, fully. Finally he got to the retirement picture, and at that moment you saw this young guy become this wizened old man. His whole life was in this shot. He went, "Hmm, hmm." Then he turned away. It was so eloquent, really set the tone of the picture. He knew he was facing death, and that's what the picture was about. All in this one shot.

MT: When you shot that shot, how much did you allow for the surprise in the actor? In other words, I can imagine Henry Fonda coming in and seeing all those pictures for the very first time. He sees what you've done and there will be one reaction. Now, the third or fourth or fifth time it might be different.

MR: He knew what the idea was. He could sense what I was trying to do. And I never told him. Just said, go admire yourself, look at your history. I placed the pictures in order, so as he went down further and further and he was looking in the mirror, he was looking even older. This is a picture about confronting death. He knew I had stated the theme of the picture in that shot. So perfect.

MT: This whole shot was your idea; it was not in the script. And with Ernest Thompson, the writer, did you suggest to him that it could be in the script, or did you just know it was something you were going to do and just left it at that?

MR: I think I knew I was going to do it and left it at that. I just arranged the pictures on the mirror and told him to go look at them one at a time.

MT: So this happened on the set on that day.

MR: Yeah, I knew what I was going to do.

MT: So being a director, you sometimes look at a scene and think, "I know what I'm going to do. I have a clear idea of what I want. And don't need to tell the writer right now, because…"

MR: It invites resistance.

MT: And are you avoiding the whole process of having to explain the shot?

MR: I talked to Henry and the writer was there. Although Katharine Hepburn didn't want him around at all. She didn't want the writer around. She did a play on Broadway of his after that, too. She admired him, but didn't want him to interfere at all. But again, this is an experience I would wish on every director, to have an experience like that. Three months in the summer with those people alone in a house on a lake. No distractions. We shot the picture practically in order because we had the cast there. I could do whatever I wanted. One house. It was a joy. What a great experience that was.

MT: How about rehearsal?

MR: I told the cast we were going to rehearse at a firehouse in the town. But when I told Katharine Hepburn she said, "I have a wonderful house. Let's all go to my house and rehearse." I thought, "Should I let her do this?" Then, "Okay, we'll go to your house." We go with her to her house a week before we're starting to shoot and she's got cookies out and we have a nice chat and there's a table set up with the scripts in front of each chair. I said, "Well, let's sit down and read," and she went to the head of the table and sat down at the head of the table and all the actors were sitting there and I knew this was the moment and my heart was beating and I said, "Kate, I think you're in my seat." She actually wanted to know who was going to direct, her or me. She moved away and sat in a side chair and I conducted rehearsal. My heart was beating a mile a minute. I was so scared she was going to say, "Fuck you, man." New story. We're about to do the first shot of the picture, a dolly shot as the car comes in. They (Katharine Hepburn and Henry Fonda) get out of the car; I keep dollying so you see the house. So, I'm setting up the dolly shot, and people are laying the track. Then Dorothy Jeakins, an Academy Award costume designer, comes to me and says, "You'd better go see what she's wearing." I said, "What do you mean? We picked all the clothes, she came to the house, tried them on." "You'd better go see what she's wearing." Remember, we haven't shot any of the picture yet. I go to the back of the house and there's the coffee table and all the stuff, buns and coffee, and she's standing there with Henry Fonda and he's in his proper outfit for having travelled from Connecticut to New Hampshire for the summer. It's their first appearance in the house and she's got on black silk pants and a black silk shirt and a fedora. She looked like Coco Chanel. So I'm standing there with Henry, she's having tea and I say, "Kate, it's time to get into wardrobe. We're getting close to the first shot." She says, "Oh, oh, this will be fine." I say, "No, no. I prefer the choice we decided on." And she says, "No, no. Don't worry, this will be fine." It was the challenge moment. I said, "Okay, everybody, let's take twenty minutes. Take a break while Ms. Hepburn gets into the proper wardrobe." I look her in the eye and she starts to quiver. She rose up imperiously, and her eyes filled with tears and Henry is standing here. I thought, here it is, this is going to be a disaster, and she whirled and walked off and went to her A-frame dressing room and Henry said, "Great, there goes the picture and we haven't made a shot yet." I said, "I don't think so." A few long minutes later she came back in the right wardrobe, angry, but in a sense relaxed, because she knew I was in charge, that I was going to direct this picture and she had to do what I said, not what she wanted, if I thought it was wrong. This was a critical moment in the making of that film. A moment of wardrobe bullshit.

MT: How much do you think she was unconsciously testing you?

MR: A lot.

MT: In that moment, she could have shut down the whole picture.

MR: Absolutely. A roll of the dice, if you want to be in charge. If you let them step on you, you'll never have control, never be able to make suggestions again for the rest of the picture. She was saying, "I'm going to run this picture." She had a lot of experience. She already had three Academy Awards. It was a critical moment.

MT: I believe that if an actor is being difficult, it is very likely fear-based. It sounds like she was afraid you wouldn't take charge and she would have to — not that she wanted to, but was afraid you wouldn't.

MR: Yes. And when I did, it didn't relieve her right away. On the surface it was a battle.

MT: Also a very public battle.

MR: In front of a lot of people. When she returned in the right wardrobe, that was the end of it. She never once questioned my judgment after that. Maybe once or twice, but never seriously. I had them in the palm of my hand.

MT: Did she ever mention it again?

MR: Months later. She said it was an important moment in the picture.

MT: On *On Golden Pond* you had two veterans.

MR: Super veterans.

MT: How was it different with Bette Midler in *The Rose?*

MR: Giant talent. Never acted before.

MT: Never acted in anything.

MR: Never.

MT: And you're putting her in the lead.

MR: But I'd seen her perform. I saw her take an audience and put them in her pocket. She was amazing. But she had never acted before. She was very intimidated by Alan Bates and these other actors who were very skilled. The first day of shooting in New York, we're at the New York Hilton, on the top floor looking out over the park. The scene was with Alan Bates and she was in a panic. There were mixed New York and L.A. crews so there was a tension there, all fighting for their position. Aaron Russo, producer, a thug, nightclub owner from Chicago, was her manager/ex-lover. Nominally a producer of the picture because he brought her to the table. We're on the top floor; the windows are gelled, looking out over the whole city. I start to walk toward her and I feel a hand on my shoulder. It's Russo.

He says, "Where are you going?"

I said, "I'm going to talk to Bette."

He said, "No, no, no. You talk to me, I talk to Bette."

"Wait a minute," I say. "Say that again."

He says, "You heard me. You don't talk to Bette. You talk to me. I talk to Bette."

So I say, "Okay, everyone gather round. Bette, come on over here."

I'm trembling. I said, "Bette, this is what just happened. I'm on my way to talk to you and he stopped me and said I don't talk to you, I talk to him and he talks to you."

The whole crew was there.

"Bette, all he can do is get you a bigger trailer. I can make you a great actress in this picture. Now you, right now, I want you to stand here and transfer all your allegiance (from her lover, by the way) to me now or you're finished and this is all over."

MT: We shut down.

MR: Yeah. She says, "Okay." I said to the cops, "Take him. Get him off the set. I don't want to see him again until the picture is finished shooting." And they took this thug off the set. It was a significant moment in the picture.

MT: And again (as with *On Golden Pond*) your decision was to do this publicly. You called in the whole crew. You could have simply made it between you and Bette.

MR: No. I wanted to say, "Let's see who's running this picture." I had to make it clear. He has no position. He's a thug. A bum. An ape. Big, fat nightclub owner who was her previous lover and at the present was her manager. But he knew nothing. He knew nightclubs and he knew muscle. I'll never forget how he held my shoulder. Those are the key moments in directing the big stars. You must, in a comfortable, supportive, friendly way, take charge. Not challenge. Genuinely say, "Look, this is what I do for a living. I tell you how it's going to go." I learned that from an interview with a conductor I saw on television in Chicago. Guy interviewing him said, "I know this will sound stupid, but what does a conductor do? What does he do? It looks like he's waving a stick. They're all playing the music, what does he do?" And the elderly conductor said, "I tell them how it's going to go. That's my job. 'This is the way it's gonna go. Go soft here.' I'm the one who tells them how it's gonna go." And I never forgot that. Really, what a director does is tells them how it's gonna go. Hopefully in a supportive and loving and affectionate way, trying to get the best out of every performer, trying to listen to all of them, encourage them to want to give you the best and include them, but be in charge. You have to be in charge. If you're not in charge, you're a dead duck. Particularly with people like Katharine Hepburn and Henry Fonda, stars of magnitude, giant stars who've had more experience than I had. If you added up the number of pictures they did as opposed to what I did. I had done only six films before I did *On Golden Pond*.

MT: But there's room for collaboration, room for an idea, room for input.

MR: I want their input. Give me everything you've got. I make it clear to them I want you to be the best you've ever been. Absolutely fascinated with what you have to give me. If I make adjustments, I'll make them gently, but come on, let's all do this together.

MT: What about the rehearsal process? I am assuming you want to rehearse as much as you can.

MR: Yes. The studio always objects. I tell them, I'm not shooting this picture without a full week around a table with the actors and they have to pay the actors for that. In some cases it's a lot of money. A weekly salary for an actor making five million, that's a lot of money. But I insist on it.

MT: What are the problems you run into in rehearsal? Do you encounter actors who don't want to rehearse, don't like to rehearse, or can't rehearse?

MR: I don't give them a choice.

"We're rehearsing. See you Monday at 10 am."

"Oh, really?"

"Yes. I'll see you then."

Then we sit around, read the material, discuss each moment, what's happening, how we feel about this or that. Get the team together. They begin to see I'm not trying to hurt them; I'm trying to help them. Most actors respond to it.

Bette was shocked when I wanted to rehearse. She was so intimidated by Alan Bates, by me, by the fact that she'd never acted for a moment. But when you saw her in the nightclub, you could see she could do anything.

The phone booth scene at the end is as good anything you're going to see on film. She was able to go deep into the darkest parts of her personality. You know, her father never saw her work. He wouldn't go.

MT: He wouldn't see the film?

MR: Never saw it. Wouldn't go see her. And I used that. The fact that she never could please her father.

MT: That's part of the character of Rose in the film, isn't it? Trying to find a connection with her father?

MR: Yes, she had wanted to prove herself to her parents.

MT: That's why she's going back to do that concert.

MR: Right. She insists on doing that concert. It's her home town and she wants to be loved by those people who humiliated her as a kid in high school. I'm looking forward to seeing the picture again on Friday night.

MT: And you used that personal part of her to help her to expose the pain of her character?

MR: I must tell you I unashamedly used it to get her motor going. Was no big job because her motor was ready to go anyway. She's got a Ferrari engine in her chest.

MT: I often ask directors: "Do you want to make a film that is limited to your imagination?"

MR: That's good.

MT: You know and I know that actors will bring magic and we will say to ourselves, "I'm using that and I'll take credit for it." And we're thinking: I had never imagined that was even possible, but there it is.

MR: Isn't that it? The creative environment in which those things can occur. You want them to occur. You don't want to lock it in. You want to see what's going to happen. It's being confident enough to know you're still in charge even if you let the actors have their way a little bit. Because who knows what's going to happen, what terrific thing could happen.

MT: Can you stay in charge and give up control?

MR: Well, you're not really giving up control.

MT: But, you're allowing the freedom for others.... .

MR: Encouraging it.

MT: Encouraging it, and a lot of directors think that being in charge is telling other people what to do.

MR: There's nothing better than creating an atmosphere in which creative people feel they have permission to flourish. That you want the best they have to offer.

Interview with
JOHN BADHAM

John Badham has earned the reputation of an "actor's director" through a career impressive in both range and diversity. In 1977, he guided a then-unknown John Travolta to worldwide fame with *Saturday Night Fever*, a cultural milestone that went on to become one of the top-grossing films of all time. Two of his early action films, *Blue Thunder* and *WarGames*, both released in 1983, received four Academy Award nominations. The American Cinematheque recently presented a 25th anniversary double feature of those two films, and Google hosted its own 25th anniversary Silicon Valley screening of *WarGames*. John is a professor at the esteemed Dodge College of Film and Media Arts at Chapman University. He is the author of *I'll Be In My Trailer: The Creative Wars Between Directors and Actors*, a brilliant examination of the delicate creative dance between directors and actors.

I had known John Badham's impressive television work and *Saturday Night Fever* long before I had the opportunity to meet him. And I knew that he and I shared a common training ground, the Yale School of Drama (YSD). We both studied under Nikos Psacharopoulos, a brilliant, energetic, and passionate director who was able to light fires in all of us. Occasionally John and I would run into each other at YSD events, but it wasn't until he was kind enough to read my first book, *The Director's Journey*, that I really began to get to know him.

After he read *The Director's Journey*, I received a phone call from John that went something like this: "Mark, do you remember what Nikos used to tell us? Remember when we would ask him 'Isn't all this stuff written down somewhere?' and he would say (in a thick Greek accent), 'It's impossible. No one can write this down. It is impossible.' Well, Mark, you've done it. Somehow you found a way to write it all down. Bless you." So of course we became great friends.

John and I met at the noisy Daily Grill in Los Angeles, perfect for a passionate discussion on directing.

MARK TRAVIS: So what about working with writers? What are some of the problems you face and how do you get around them?

JOHN BADHAM: I believe that — as much as possible — that when you, the director, discover something that bothers you in the screenplay, that you should think of some kind of solution to it, two or three solutions that you can present to the writer. Something more than "I don't like this part" or "This scene isn't very good." Be specific about whose point of view it is, or that the objectives aren't clear or the conflict is non-existent. Be specific and say, "What if?" For example, in *Stakeout*, Richard Dreyfuss spends the whole time pretending to Madeline Stowe that he's a telephone repairman while he's actually a police officer who's spying on her. They kind of develop a thing for each other and she still thinks he's a telephone repairman. And the screenplay keeps dancing around this little farcical premise, so I finally said to Jim Kouf, the writer, "We're dancing around this. What happens if we just face up to this dilemma? What happens if she finds out? Isn't that good dramatic fodder?" And he lit up and said, "Well, yeah, that's good." Sometimes you feel writers have some kind of plot device going and they're afraid of letting it topple, whereas toppling often leads to much more interesting stuff.

MT: So you felt like he was playing it safe?

JB: Yeah, I felt like he had it in his mind that he didn't want to cross over that bridge. But there are some times I find in directing, action scenes in particular, you often find yourself blocking ideas because you're not willing to play it logically. What would happen if the bad guy actually got to this woman as she's running out of the garage? And that's when you start coming up with really interesting solutions.

MT: Because you've created a bigger problem.

JB: You've created a much bigger problem.

MT: Which is much more exciting for the audience because we don't know how you're going to get out of it. Like with *Stakeout*, I'm guessing the writer's fear is if Richard Dreyfuss reveals who he is, then it will all fall apart.

JB: The whole story falls apart.

MT: Your solution to the problem might be much more interesting than the original script. If you let the characters get into trouble and you commit to helping them fight their way through, the results might be much more interesting.

JB: Right. And, in fact, what happens in the screenplay is she (Madeline Stowe) has a complete fit and Richard's trying to explain that he wasn't using her, that maybe it started that way but it has gone another way, and she doesn't want to hear it and we all get that, right? We all get it. And so he had brought their relationship to the point where they were really falling for each other, and now you pull them apart. Standard "boy meets girl, boy gets girl, boy loses girl." On *Saturday Night Fever* I did a lot of work with Norman Wexler, the author. He had a 160-page draft that they were talking about shooting, and I'm thinking, "This is not going to fly."

And they're saying, "Oh, by the way, we start shooting in two weeks." So my feeling at this point is that the writer is so close to the material that he really needs somebody to come in with very specific notes such as: "Cut this section, cut this down, why don't you try it this way, what if you do it like this?" I had to get the script down to a reasonable length, which I thought was about 115 pages. A lot of stuff had to be chucked out the window, but you still had plenty of screenplay.

MT: So you went in and edited it? You made the cuts?

JB: I made the cuts and then I would say to the writer, "I know we're busy and I'm a terrible writer — I'm no good at all, but I had some ideas and rather than sit here and blab about them to you, I put them into an easy to understand form. If you hate them, by all means, throw them out. It's okay. You won't hurt my feelings (lie, lie, lie). My ego won't be hurt. And so I give him the script marked up relatively neatly and that way I hope to take some of the pressure off. He may be thinking, "This guy's forcing me to do something really stupid which I think would be wrong." That does seem to work pretty well, rather than laying it all on him. And then he might use some of it and maybe it gives him an insight on something else, a fresh perspective. But whenever I can come up with specific suggestions, even if it's dialogue, I say, "This is a terrible idea, but what if the guy says, and please don't use these words, 'Blah, blah, blah.'" And it's the best I can come up with at the time. And the writer might say, "No, no, no — this is what you want to say." Now his greater skills as a writer start to take over. I've always been able to work pretty well with writers that way.

MT: Part of the trick is the self-deprecation: "Listen, I'm not a writer. This is badly written, but here's the idea."

JB: One thing you have to remember: It's easy for you to read the words on the page in a few minutes, but the writer spent a lot of time, whether he dashed it out in two weeks or six months. He's made specific choices for specific reasons and it's hard to let go of them. It's an emotional connection unless you're lucky enough to have someone who can detach enough to not have fallen in love with every paragraph.

MT: How do you work with actors in the casting process?

JB: Well, one thing I can tell you is whatever you feel about the character, do not waste your time telling the actor any of it because the actor has sat out there and thought out his own plans and he's going to do it the way he thought of it. If you're so foolish as to say, "You know, here's a character who's trying to do such and such," you just wasted your breath. The actor isn't going to listen to a word you say because he's planned it one way. Now after they do it you can say, "Okay, pretty good. What if you were to try it..." and that's the time to give them the adjustment, whatever it is they need. They're not ready to hear it before then. I'm a great believer in getting up from the table and going over and shaking the actor's hand when they come in. A lot of times I just want to sit there, but I make myself get up and go over there and start some bonding with the actors. I think this is critical to getting them relaxed enough to read the part. That's another thing with the first time through — you're watching whatever their performance is with a layer of fear and tension on top of it. And they may have to do it two or three times before it starts to settle down. And then there are plenty of people who never do settle down. They're too tense, too frightened.

MT: What do you do besides going over and talking to them? How valuable do you think it is to get to know them more personally?

JB: (Elia) Kazan believed that it's absolutely critical that you take them to coffee or lunch and spend time with them. It's not only to get to be friends with them, but to find out what makes this human being tick. And what kind of life history they have. He says, very clearly, actors are the easiest people to get information from because they love to talk about themselves and their history. They'll just jump right out there and tell you stuff none of the rest of us would utter with a subpoena. That gives you the added knowledge which you can use when you're doing the scenes because you have a little of their own personal backstory and how they relate to it. (In episodic television) we only get to say hello to the cast during prep. No real opportunities to go out to dinner and talk. But make use of any time you can spend with them. I'm a great believer in arriving at the set half an hour before call and going in the make-up trailer and talking to whatever actors are there at that hour. "How's it going? What do you think of the scenes today? Do you have any problems?" I know they probably studied that scene late last night, or early this morning, and they're just starting to think about it for the first time. Or they read it a couple of days ago, but didn't really think about it. And now they're thinking, "Oh my God. I have to say this and I have to do that and how am I going to do that?" So, I'd rather spend a few minutes with them in the make-up trailer than spend it out on the set when everyone's looking at their watches.

MT: This leads to another issue. Safety. I believe it's our job as directors to create a safe environment for the actors within which they can work. And if we don't create that safe environment, then their creativity is severely restricted or hampered.

JB: That's right. I just say flat out, "It's okay to fail. Screwing up is perfectly okay. It's not okay to come to the set and not

know your lines or to not have thought about the character. But if in the middle of saying 'To be or not to be' you
decide to do back flips, then I want you to go do back flips.
The worst that can happen is we decide to do it without the
back flips. But what if it's amazingly good? You should not
be censoring yourself. It won't piss me off. We can always do
it again." Even though you're under great pressure for time
and the production manager part of you says, "Don't do this!
This is insane!," it actually is very settling and calming and
helps people loosen up. Making a safe environment makes
people totally relax, and if people aren't totally relaxed, then
their imagination can't start to work. The more relaxed you
are, the more your imagination is going. And the more tense
you are… Stanislavsky was doing exercises about this, how
adding tension can completely destroy an actor's work.

MT: What are your thoughts about rehearsal?

JB: I am a great believer in rehearsal, because that's where
you have the opportunity to explore more than what's on
the page, where you have a chance to try different things. If
someone wants to do back flips, there's no problem at all. Or
if they want to do it in some really peculiar way, that's the
time. Or if they have a problem with the scene, or they don't
like the scene. If you haven't rehearsed and you get to staging
the scene and now they come up with "I hate this scene,"
then you've got to make a quick decision, think of something. I'd rather have a little more time to think about that
decision. At the same time, there are some actors who just
do not like to rehearse. They want to just learn lines and go.
Mel Gibson's one of those people. He'll come out and stage
the scene, but if you're looking for any indication of what
the performance is going to be like, forget it. You're going
to get mumbling and barely saying the lines — he does
know them — but it can give you a heart attack because

you're thinking, "Is this what this scene's going to be like?" Then you roll and you go for it and suddenly this whole other person emerges who's this whimsical, wicked little imp who has all these funny little things he's been holding onto.

MT: Only when the camera's rolling?

JB: Yep. He saves all of that stuff. He likes to keep it fresh. Now, he has an unbelievable level of relaxation and a good imagination, so he can get away with that. Other people are much more methodical. I remember working with Hal Holbrook, whose Mark Twain (his one-man show, *Mark Twain Tonight*) is so carefully, methodically thought out. But that works for him.

There's no right way or wrong way to do this stuff. At the end of the day, does the scene work or doesn't it work? If it doesn't work and the actor did everything 'right,' well then it's bullshit. Something's wrong here, the scene doesn't work. But if the scene's fabulous and he did everything 'wrong,' then it's okay. You can't criticize the actor for not doing it in the 'right' Stanislavsky method if the scene is good. Who cares? It's really okay.

MT: What did you do with the other actors; the one's who aren't the stars? For example, if I'm an actor working with Mel Gibson and I know I'm not going to get a rehearsal, what are you telling me? What are you as a director doing to help these actors?

JB: This is when you're glad you cast really good, experienced actors who can be relaxed and can absorb what he's doing as things are going on. He's very quick and very flexible, and if the other actors are that way, as Goldie Hawn (in *Bird On a Wire*) was — she tends to be more set in her performances, but she's also cool enough that she can change to meet the circumstances. You can say to the actors, "You may have noticed that we don't get much out of him, but he'll be there on the day, so just respond. If something goes wrong or different, just deal with it and see how it goes. It's not your fault if you mess up, or if you get an idea you want to try and it doesn't work out. It's okay." Again, you're just trying to relax the actors.

MT: How much are you aware that you're a psychologist or a parent on the set, day in and day out?

JB: I think you're always aware of it. And I think you're aware that every single person on the set is a totally different human being with different approaches and there's no unified way of approaching a scene or acting a scene. Your main strategy is making them feel comfortable and treating them with respect as adults, even if what you're getting back is childish and immature. You have to hang onto these principles. These are techniques and strategies to keep the set relaxed. Read a book called *PET — Parent Effectiveness Training*. You'll learn more techniques for working with actors, and the book is talking about children. It works with adults, it works with anybody. I recommend this book. It's wonderful.

MT: One last question having to do with production. You're shooting the actress in a scene, it's a key moment, and you feel you've got it. You have what you need. She says, "No, there's more" or "I need to do it again." My question isn't about shooting it again. My question is about convincing the actors, and even yourself, that you do have the scene. I will almost always, if possible, give the actor one more take. But then what I will do is say, "You're right. There was something there. Thank you." And I may have seen nothing new. It may have been exactly the same, but they feel validated. And I'm off the hook.

JB: That's a great idea.

MT: That's the psychology, the PET — dealing with the "child."

JB: We're such manipulative assholes, we directors.

MT: Yes, we are. But we love it, John.

JB: This is the kind of work that keeps me going after forty years — finding solutions to the challenges and problems. I look forward to having interesting encounters with actors and trying to figure out how to make it work better. And when I actually can make it better, it's great. And a lot of times I can't make it better, I can only make it different.

Interview with
WILL MACKENZIE

Will Mackenzie has received six Emmy nominations for outstanding direction of the television series *Scrubs, Everybody Loves Raymond, Family Ties*, and *Moonlighting*. He also won the Directors Guild Award for the *Moonlighting* episode "Atomic Shakespeare," based on Shakespeare's *The Taming of the Shrew*, and the one-hour episode of *Family Ties* called "A. My Name is Alex." He has directed theatre and many other TV series, including *Newhart, WKRP in Cincinnati, Dharma & Greg*, and *Reba*.

Born in Providence, Rhode Island, Will graduated from Brown University and received a Fulbright Scholarship to the London Academy of Music and Drama. As an actor he appeared on Broadway in *Hello Dolly* opposite Carol Channing, Ginger Rogers, Betty Grable, and Martha Raye, *Half A Sixpence* opposite Tommy Steele, *Much Ado About Nothing* with Sam Waterston, and the tours of *Promises, Promises* and *The Apple Tree* with his wife of 44 years, Patricia Cope Mackenzie. He played "Larry Bondurant" on *The Bob Newhart Show*, which led to his first directing assignment in television 35 years ago.

In all my years of shadowing sitcom directors, and then eventually directing *Family Ties* and *The Facts of Life*, I was always aware of, and in awe of, Will Mackenzie. It seemed like he was everywhere, directing everything. I used to see him from a distance at DGA events and screenings, but never approached him.

But a few months ago we ran into each other at yet another DGA function and I was bold enough to introduce myself. I was shocked and honored that he knew me and knew something of my career. But then, when he enthusiastically agreed to be interviewed for this book, I was thrilled.

Will and I met at the popular Chin Chin restaurant in Studio City, CA.

WILL MACKENZIE: I think most directors who do well in film and television have come out of theatre, have done some theatre. Otherwise, how are you really going to be comfortable with actors if you haven't had a theatre background?

MARK TRAVIS: Do you have a theatre background?

WM: Yes. I was an actor for a long time. A lot of Broadway shows, mostly musicals. And then sort of lucked into getting some Summer Stock directing. I knew I wasn't going to stay being an actor my entire career. Having been an actor, I think that helped me, made the big difference. Once I got directing actors, I wasn't afraid of them, but I also respected them, knew how hard it was and what it took to get a really, really good performance, and I also knew the directors I liked, the kind of atmosphere they created. I studied with Sandy Meisner for two-and-a-half years. Best thing I learned from him is the repetition game. It's getting the actor to listen, pay attention, and either be annoyed or provoked. His big thing was independent activities — the activity that is independent of the conversation, so that if you're having a scene that is tragic — talking about the death of your mother — and you're pouring soy sauce on something and it spills all over the table — he juxtaposed the dialogue with some sort of comic business, or you have some very serious business and you're doing a very funny scene. That to me is one of the key things when you're directing television, especially four-camera television. One of the big things I've learned, though, is that you always have to be on the side of the actor. You can't let the actor think you are an extended writer on the show. They won't trust you nearly as much. They want to know that you're part of their team, not the other team. No matter how agreeable the show, there's always a writer's camp and an actor's camp. One of the classic things I remember, an actor named Barnard Hughes, he was like a father figure to me, one of my closest friends. I was an actor on *The Bob Newhart Show* and that was one of the first shows I ever directed. Barney Hughes, who was at the time one of the prime character actors, played Bob's father. He wasn't that old, maybe sixty, and he couldn't remember a couple of lines. I said to the writers, "When an actor of Barnard Hughes' stature can't remember lines, I find it's the lines that are the problem, not the actor." And I still find that to be true. Having been an actor was the best stepping stone to becoming a director. I find a lot of writers are good directors, too, having written the material. They start realizing it's not as easy as it looks playing these parts, saying some of these stupid lines that they've been given, without any reality. Basically, with all these shows, I start by grinding it into reality. I don't try for laughs or any of that stuff.

MT: How do you deal with the writers, if you're trying to help the actors, to help them get around the problem as you see it, or as the actors see it?

WM: That's a very good question. You have to find a way to convince them that it's really hurting their show if they're just keeping the line in for a laugh and there's nothing that leads up to it. On *Family Ties*, Gary (producer/creator Gary David Goldberg) would be the first person to cut a joke if it wasn't real and right for the show. *Everybody Loves Raymond* was successful because they were grounded in reality. Definitely a heightened reality.

MT: How do you conduct the casting process when you're bringing a guest actor into a well-oiled machine, like a hit sitcom?

WM: I'm looking to make that person as comfortable as possible. Having been an actor, I go out of my way to make sure that the regular cast is nice to that person, give that person more time. I talk to the guest star and make them feel comfortable, because I want their work to be good and up to par with everybody else… especially if it's a fairly big guest star part. I've seen too many situations where the actor feels like 'I'm only here for this week and I really don't care.'

MT: What are some of the challenges you face in rehearsal? What tricks do you use?

WM: *Sense of Direction* (by William Ball) is the best book on directing I've read, and have given it to so many young directors. His trick is to give the actor the first three ideas that they have. Eventually a smart actor will realize if it's a stupid idea, and sometimes if you think it's a stupid idea maybe it's a good idea for him. When I went into *Moonlighting*, it was a big show, not a hit yet. It was the first season and Cybill Shepherd was a big star then, and Bruce Willis was a nobody. On the first day of shooting I gave Cybill a piece of business that she loved. She is quite self-conscious in many ways. I helped her and I gave her some business she liked. My friend Jeff Bleckner (director) said, "Go right in and find something that will help her." And then she talked to Bruce Willis, because he had a different scene later in the day. She said to him, "You're going to love this guy, he's really good" and that broke the wall with Bruce. And then, of course, I had a terrific piece of business for him which, if he didn't want to do it, that's fine. I can't even remember what the business was. I do remember that he said, "Yeah, that's a good idea. Let me try that." You give this stuff to Michael J. Fox (*Family Ties*), he'd come over and kiss you. He is the most grateful actor.

MT: Giving them the first three ideas they come up with and giving them something to make them feel comfortable, an independent activity... these are tricks. You're helping them get past their discomfort.

WM: Right. And I've worked with so many actors who've never acted before. They're usually pretty little girls, or handsome young men. We had one on *Reba*, a sweet, sweet girl, but she didn't know what she was doing. She would say a line, but didn't know what to do with her hands. We had a little boy on there, too, who would stand there at attention and recite his lines. You have to give them something so that they're focusing on drinking the tea, for instance, rather than saying their lines.

MT: In production, how do you manage those actors who freeze up or shut down, or get uptight or nervous simply because the camera's there?

WM: Sometimes you have to go back and give them a different piece of business or a different thought about how they can read the line.

MT: How can you tell if an actor has a sense of humor and can handle comedy?

WM: Meredith (Baxter) is a perfect example. She would laugh three times when you tell her a joke. The first time when you tell it to her, the second time when you explain it to her, and the third time when she understands it. She could be funny if you explained it to her. So often she wouldn't get it, but she was grounded in such reality. Patricia Heaton *(Everybody Loves Raymond)*, who is grounded in reality, is one of the funniest people you'd ever want to meet. Doris Roberts is a comic actress. Patricia can do anything. You've got to get on the side of the actors, have to get them with you. Patricia really helped Ray, because he's a stand-up, and stand-ups get laughs. That's

the love they feel. Ray Romano was smart enough to realize that if his show was to succeed, he had to be believable,
a good actor. Every season he would get better and better,
mostly because he would work the scenes with Patricia Heaton over and over. He learned a lot about listening, about
behavior. Ray was really the core of that show. He took it
seriously. In his defense, the show was about his life. He and
Phil Rosenthal sort of combined the Italian with the Jew-
ish ethnic thing. That was Ray's life. He lived at home until
he married Anna. And his brother was a policeman. That
framed the entire show.

Interview with
JAN ELIASBERG

Jan Eliasberg is a director, screenwriter, and novelist. She began directing film as the recipient of a grant from the American Film Institute's Directing Workshop for Women. Her film *The Doctor*, starring Lukas Haas, won many festival awards and attracted the attention of Michael Mann, who hand-picked Jan to be the first woman to direct the iconic *Miami Vice* and *Crime Story*, as well as *Wiseguy* and *21 Jump Street*.

She has directed dramatic pilots for series at CBS, ABC, and NBC, as well as the film *Past Midnight*, starring Paul Giamatti, for New Line Cinema. Jan has received the Dorothy Arzner Award, the NAACP Award, and the Imagen Award.

Jan holds an MFA in Directing from the Yale School of Drama, where she directed some of the greatest American actors of her generation: Frances McDormand, Angela Bassett, Tony Shalhoub, Paul Giamatti, and John Turturro. She has taught screenwriting, directing and fiction at USC, UCLA, the Art Institute of California, Bennington Writer's Conference, Wesleyan Writer's Conference, and was a guest artist at the Sundance Institute. She has been a consultant for the National Endowment for the Arts and the New York State Council on the Arts.

Many times I will attend the monthly meetings of the Alameda Writer's Group (AWG) in Glendale, CA. Besides the opportunity to meet with many accomplished writers, AWG offers some of the best guest speakers (Dara Marks, John Truby and my good friend, the late Blake Snyder). Several months ago I was attending one of these meetings and the guest speaker was talking about breaking into the film and television industry and how you might need the support and skills of a mentor or coach (a service she was offering). Then she asked a friend and colleague of hers to talk for a few minutes about the challenges of directing television: Jan Eliasberg. As soon as Jan started talking, my ears perked up. Here was a woman speaking my language. Then, of course, when she mentioned that she had studied at the Yale School of Drama, it all became clear. At the conclusion of the event I cornered Jan, quickly introduced myself, told her of our shared training at YSD, and insisted that we have lunch sometime soon.

At a casual lunch several weeks later we shared war stories, artistic challenges, Yale experiences, swapped screenplays we had written, and Jan enthusiastically agreed to be part of my new book.

MARK TRAVIS: Jan, let's start with writers. Do you have any specific thoughts about working with writers?

JAN ELIASBERG: Yes, of course, I have a lot of thoughts about working with writers. One of the things I always find challenging is that I am a writer myself, so when I go in as a director, I often will go in with a lot of my ideas about how I would write the script or change the script. The big trick for me is to figure out how to get the writer to think it's his or her idea as opposed to my idea, and actually I should say that's not always the case. Sometimes I will form a bond with the writer quickly… you know, as a director, particularly working in television, my feeling is that you have to assess things very, very quickly, whether it's with the writer, with the crew, or with an actor. I will try very quickly to have my radar out, and I will always try to have a very candid, very frank conversation about usually nothing… your kids, where they went to school. I want to find out is this a writer who's going to be hanging on to every word, which means it's going to necessitate one kind of approach, or is this a writer who really is open to collaboration? I've worked with both. There was one case where I had a writer who was very open to collaboration and I literally walked in with Post-Its hanging off every single page of the script, and he was like, "Uh-oh, let's get to work!" But I knew already that he'd be open. Would never do that with a writer who I sense is going to be resistant. I've been on some shows where there are writers on the set who literally have the script in front of their nose. They're not watching the actors, they're not watching the monitor, and when the take is finished, they've got their head phones in and the script in front of their face and they're like, 'that was great.' And you're like, "That fucking sucked." They just want to know if every word was uttered. Because that's what they care about. They don't care about the reality or the emotional vulnerability. Or, 'of course she skipped that line because she was in the moment and it didn't come out perfectly,' but that's what's going to end up in the cut if you have an editor with half a brain.

MT: In fact, it might be the skipped line, because she was so in the moment, she organically....

JE: Made a better line. And it's sad, because you would hope they're looking for some life and vitality. The writers are so different in terms of their sensitivity or their sense of what they're looking for, and some writers really do feel that every word is precious, and some writers are good enough that every word *is* precious. They've really thought it through that way. So, as a director, I try to sense that pretty early, too. Because some writers do really think things through on that level. I've found that the more I can sort of let the writer know early on that I'm there to make the best show possible and I'm not doing it at their expense, that we're on the same team, the more they'll say, "These are really good notes." Because they can see they're going to make the script better and they haven't had time to think all of this through.

MT: In your work with story and script and writers, how much do you think your theatre background has helped you?

JE: Oh, immensely. My theatre background, and specifically my training at Yale, is actually the template for everything I still do. In those three years at Yale, I directed over sixty plays in different stages: cabaret, workshop reading, full reading, and some of those were the great plays of the canon and some were fresh off some writer's typewriter or computer. But, doing that and doing so much of it so quickly with actors of a very high caliber, whether it was Frances McDormand or John Turturro or Angela Bassett, actors who were going to ask the hard questions. It just threw me into the swimming pool so many times that there isn't really any situation that I don't, in some instinctive way, know how to deal with.

MT: So, that boot camp that you were talking about — where you were thrown into so many theatre challenges — has become a valuable tool, because you develop survive tools. I keep telling my film students, "Theatre is harder."

JE: Film is much easier because of the technology. You also have a whole crew that knows what they're doing, that knows those machines inside and out, that knows all the tricks, that can help you if you understand what story you're telling. You can talk about what the moments are and why you're interested in dollying in on this moment. They'll make it work, better than you ever could, probably. But the other thing I always remember is that when you're in a rehearsal room for a month with those kinds of actors, then they're asking you hard questions and they're trying to piece together what they need to make the performance work. So when you talk about motivation or objectives or given circumstances, it's not technique to me. It's the way you figure out what's going on in the scene. And then, a thing like blocking, I will always go into a scene, even a badly written scene, trying to figure out how to block it in a way that gets the emotional arc of the scene across. So then I think, "Okay, now that I've got the blocking in this organic way, how do I integrate the camera into that so that the camera is seeing what I want the audience to see?" I don't think I would be a good director without that training.

MT: Mark Rydell once said: "Filmmaking is easy. You create an event. You record the event. And then you reorganize the recording of the event to create a third event. But if the first event isn't worth recording, then I don't know what you're doing."

JE: And I would only add one thing: I don't want to record the event. I want the camera in some way to participate in the event. In my mind, the event will usually tell me how it needs to be recorded.

MT: Absolutely.

JE: And that sounds very new-agey and artsy-fartsy, like Michelangelo, you know — "the stone tells me what it wants to be" — but that has been my experience. And I experience auditions in that way very much, and we'll go back to your tricks question. I will always use the audition to show the writer what's working and what's not working.

MT: And how do you do that?

JE: Well, I will see maybe three actors and I'll see the same moment not working and I'll be able to say, "Gee, that

moment isn't resonating. And now we've seen three wonderful actors do it and they've hit all these other moments.
I wonder if that maybe is a moment that isn't quite there."
You can blame an actor once, twice, but if you've got three
actors and they're all missing the same beat, then maybe
it's not the actors. Maybe it's a problem in the script.

MT: So you have the writer there during casting?

JE: Yes.

MT: In the casting process, what tricks do you use with the
actors?

JE: Well, I always say that casting is my first opportunity to
rehearse. Especially with episodic, because it's happening so
quickly... I may not even have gotten the script very far in
advance. So casting is my first chance to hear something read
aloud. And, a lot of times, through seeing actors, I'm finding
the strengths and weaknesses in the scene. So a lot of times
when I give direction in casting, which I always do, if I don't
see anything that's interesting, I say, "Thank you very much."
If I see something interesting in an actor, I will always give
them some kind of adjustment. Sometimes because I really
want to see the actor work with something, but sometimes
just because I want to see what's in the scene and the actor's
given me something I didn't know was there and I just want
to explore that a little bit and see, well, if I take the scene in
that direction in performance, how far can I go with that?

MT: A lot of the tricks I talk about in casting have to do
with being aware of the mindset of the actors. In other
words, I've got an actress in front of me reading and I know
she wants the job, she wants the job so much she'd probably
do almost anything I ask her to. The same actress probably
won't be so compliant in rehearsal as she slowly becomes

the character. And in production she is the character and she has a job to do. In casting, I can ask her to do the scene in a totally inappropriate way just to see is she skilled enough and courageous enough to pull it off? I may say something like, "This argument scene with your husband is really a seduction and I need to see it now." If she gives me the same reading she gave before, then I don't have much to work with. So, Jan, in the casting, putting aside the material, are you testing them?

JE: That's interesting. It really depends on what the situation is for me. If I'm proving myself as a director and I've got producers who are thinking, "Is she going to be able to give us what we need?" I probably don't have as much room to do that stuff because they'll go, "What is she thinking? She's got this argument scene and she's asking them to do it as a seduction. Uh-oh, she's really off base and we've got to talk to her and get her in a tone meeting." If I have more freedom on shows that I create, or on shows where they've worked with me a lot and they know that I do deliver, then absolutely. In fact, the more I can treat everything as play, the better.

MT: By play you mean....

JE: By play I mean: Let's try it and have fun. Let's try it and see if it works. There aren't any mistakes here. You know, I just had a great idea... I know this sounds crazy, but let's play. That's what I mean by play, because the more I get that feeling, of like, we can go to these places that might be scary... you know, let's just take the anxiety out of the process as much as possible. Let's forget that we have to get to this goal. Let's just play. The more there's that spirit, the better the work is, in my experience. And the more the actors lose that self-consciousness, which is the thing that gets in the way of a really fresh performance.

MT: One thing you just mentioned is my 'insanity trick,' where I say to an actor... and this could be in any phase — casting, rehearsal, or production — "Listen, I've got this idea. I'm sure it's totally insane. I'm sure it's not going to work, but..." Which means I'm going to take all the blame. All I'm asking them to do is think about it, and if it doesn't work, well, I was right, it was insane, or it was impossible.

JE: Yep. I do that, too. I always put the pressure on me. Always. Because I feel like that's my job. I'm the parent, and when I say "Play," I feel like the set is a sandbox. And if everybody feels like there's a parent in charge who's going to make sure sand doesn't get in the eyes, or if it does then it's flushed out, but if there's a parent in charge then everyone can play and those moments of fear are short and brief. So my job is to let people know that I'm a parent, I'm a good parent, and I'm going to protect them. If they look stupid — my fault. If I ask them to try something and it works, great, they get all the credit. If it doesn't work, it was a really stupid idea. And I'll say sometimes, "You know, that really sucked. Whose stupid idea was that?" And everybody will laugh, and then the next take will be great because I've sort of taken the onus of responsibility on me and I've made it okay to do something really dumb. It's generally out of those risky things that the really great moments come. When everyone's playing, it's safe. And sort of hitting all their marks and hitting all the beats. It can get lifeless. And my job in those moments is to do something to mix it up. Doesn't even have to be the right thing. I'll say — it's just like your trick of counting to five before saying the line — I'll say, "I just want to drive this scene. I don't want any pauses, I don't want any air, I just want you to barrel through this." "Why?" "Just because." Things happen. So, that's one trick I'll use. Or, a lot of times I'll take actors aside and tell them to do something that I won't share with the other actor that is sometimes very intense. I'll say, if it's a goodbye scene, for instance, "Just find a moment in this scene to touch her cheek. Or just find something you just love about her and touch her there." The other actor is usually shocked... and that reaction is usually a great moment.

MT: And suddenly the whole focus of the character has changed, and the scene changes, and a magical moment may happen during the looking for the moment.

JE: Or, to the other actor when it happens. It's like, "What? What was going on there?"

MT: And these are perfect, Jan, because these get the actors past their barriers and sometimes the barrier is the fact that we've been shooting the scene all day and they've got nothing new. And now it's their close up. I need them to shift what's going on internally, to get them on a track without saying, "Get back on track."

JE: And that's why I think objectives are really important and action words. If I can shift the objective, even to something that makes no sense, then the scene is going to be fresh. That I know. I worked with Rutger Hauer, who was wonderful at this. He would nail a scene and then he'd say, "Give me something else to do with it." And I would, and he would, and that's where I sort of get this idea of play, because what I ended up with in the editing room... he was a character that you were never supposed to be quite sure about. I ended up with all of these takes that were really different, and I could actually use moments from one, moments from the other, where he would go from being very, very sort of compassionate and intent and sweet to being really quite dangerous.

MT: And in production?

JE: One of my big tricks is actually not talking to the actor who's on-camera, but talking to the actor who's off-camera.

MT: About what?

JE: Changing the objective. Or asking that actor to do something different because I'm trying to elicit a reaction from the actor who's on-camera but I don't want to make that actor self-conscious by asking him to do something specific, so I use my off-camera actor to make it happen. If you keep giving adjustments to the actor who's on-camera, he starts to feel like 'I must not be getting it because the director keeps coming up and talking to me' and sometimes that can be very anxiety-producing. It's like 'what am I doing wrong?' Where I'm just looking for a little bit of a different approach or a little bit of a different moment. But if I'm talking to the actors off-camera, somehow the actors on-camera are just reacting, the honest genuine reaction, which is what you want.

MT: Do you ever have the actor off-camera say something different than their lines?

JE: Yes.

MT: And what has your experience been with that?

JE: It depends on how good the actor who's on-camera is. If the actor is really green, they'll get totally thrown and you might get a great moment in the instant, but then it all falls apart. If the actor's really there, then a lot of times that can be great and the scene can go in completely different directions. I'll also do things with physicality or, sometimes I'll even do it myself if a scene seems to be falling into a rut, I'll start saying things from off-camera: "Say it again! I don't believe you!" Things like that.

MT: Just to stimulate them.

JE: Yes. "I don't believe you. Go back to something and convince me!" Again, there's got to be a trust there.

MT: Yes, and your knowledge of the actor's ability to handle that.

JE: Yes, and an actor who's done theatre will take that and run with it.

MT: Getting back to television rehearsal for a moment. How much rehearsal do you get?

JE: Almost none.

MT: So you're rehearsing on the set, in production?

JE: Pretty much.

MT: So how do you get what you want?

JE: I always ground the scene. I always have a rehearsal with the actors without the crew. Pretty much for every scene unless the scene is a total throwaway, because I always want the actors to feel they are the priority. You talk about creating an event; I don't want the event to be about the crew. I mean an action sequence, yes, the event is about the stunts and the crew. I've thought it through and I've storyboarded it, but if it's a scene about the actors, I want the event to be about the actors and that starts with let's just read through this, let's not even block it right now, let's just read through it because that's when the questions come up. When I can ask questions like, "You talk about this in the scene. What was that? Was it a big fight? A little fight? When did you guys meet?" That's when I can ground the scene in the given circumstances. And again, I'll say this is sort of my theory of play — 'let's sketch something in' and usually, my blocking, I try to keep as organic as possible, which is hard. So, I'll try to have a certain number of props there that I'm thinking I can probably use to give me some motivation for blocking and staging. I've got a shape of the scene in my head.

Then I'll talk to the actors after we've read it and grounded the scene in the circumstances and done some work on motivation, not character work. I assume they've done the character work on their own, and certainly if there's anything major about character, I've talked with them. Then I'll shape a scene like molding clay. I don't want it to get too stuck, but I want to start to give it a shape. Then I'll have the DP there and we'll be watching what the actors are doing and I'll be suggesting, "Oh, you know. It feels like you want to move away from her. Why don't you go and get this piece of paper that I've cleverly placed in the desk over here. And here it is!" Usually actors will respond to that. Some actors are like "Just tell me what to do," and then I'll tell them what to do. But I'd rather a scene evolve organically if it can. Then, as I'm watching with the DP, I usually have thoughts about how I'm going to cover it, and which moments are important, but I'll also watch how things are flowing. And then we do a marking rehearsal for the crew and then I'll refine it with the second team. Usually not with first team, because first team has a lot of other things to do — they're learning their lines and getting make-up on, and also I don't want the actor to be too much a part of that technical process, because they're starting to think, "I've got to hit my mark."

MT: One line you said, "Looks like you want to move away from her." This is a trick. At least by my definition. You're planting an idea in the mind of the actor that may never have been there. But you are saying that you are getting that impulse from him, giving him credit. He may be thinking: "Oh, it looked that way? Really? Okay, I guess I do."

JE: Totally.

MT: Sometimes inferring that the actor is doing something or has the impulse to do something is much more powerful and effective than asking the actor to do that very same thing.

JE: A lot of times the actor is reacting in a specific way, but they are stifling the impulse. Perhaps the impulse that I see in that moment is, 'Oh, I don't like that' and then I'll respond with, "Oh, it looks like you want to move away from her in that moment."

MT: On top of that you have that mechanical move (blocking) that they can do to fulfill that impulse, which is 'why don't you go over there and get that piece of paper, which is important for your character.' Now you've given them a mechanical move, but the actor also knows why he's making that move: 'Because I don't want to be near her.' So what's been inserted in the scene is an emotional response and you've given a mechanical expression of that response.

JE: And that's why I always say props animate it, props make a scene. A well-chosen prop, if there's a conflict, will become the source of the conflict. There are keys. Who's got the keys? She's got them in her hand. She throws them at him. He puts them down. She takes them away. He grabs them back. And suddenly the scene is about keys, but I've just found the source of the conflict that you then hopefully see on film.

MT: Any last words to aspiring directors?

JE: Act, yourself. Even if it's just in a little showcase or a scene. Or take an acting class, because if you've acted yourself, you know how vulnerable an actor is, and you know what kind of direction helps and what kind of direction doesn't help. So, that's one thing. Second, do your homework as much as you can, because things like having those props there require you to have thought about what is really going on in this scene. Those props don't get there by accident.

You have to ask for them. And where does that come from? It comes from really analyzing what's going on in the scene. What are the character's objectives? Where are they coming from? Where are they going? And then trust your intuition. If you think something's not working... I mean some of the best moments for me are when I can see an actor struggling and I know they are going for something and I don't even know what it is. I just feel like there's something there, and I walk over because I feel like, 'They need me. They need me to say something.' And I will literally walk over, not even knowing what I am going to say. Just knowing I have to say something, and whatever comes out of my mouth usually produces a great result. But it's not because I planned it... I guess if I hadn't had the experiences I've had (directing theatre), I might not have all those instincts. One of the tricks I learned as a director was every single job I got I saw as a learning opportunity. Early in my career I was offered things that weren't that good, they really weren't great. Television, film, anything. So I would challenge myself to find something to learn from the experience. I don't know if this fits into your book at all, but it may be tricks for directors, certainly a trick for me, was: 'I'm going to give myself a parameter. This show is going to be about moving camera. Every single shot is going to move. This show is going to be about lenses. I'm not going to use a zoom. I'm going to determine lens size for every single shot because I want to give myself this spine, and in a way that's like saying to the actor 'go get that piece of paper' or 'touch her.' How am I going to challenge myself to keep this fresh for me, so that everything I'm doing is fresh.

MT: And what inspires these boundaries?

JE: Usually I would say that I probably come up with the boundaries because of something I sense in the material. Usually they're not arbitrary.

MT: It's an instinct.

JE: It's an instinct. For instance, something in the script reminds me of a specific film. I go and watch that film, and I look at the director's work and I think, "Oh, it's the director's style, lot of steadicam. Or, this is almost a documentary style." The task isn't imposed in some arbitrary way. It's coming out of the story, because the story is everything. Telling that story in the best way possible, that is the goal.

EXERCISES:

Now you have heard from six very skilled directors who were willing to share their experiences with you. The question is, what did you learn from them?

Each of these directors is sharing tricks, so for each director here is what I want you to do.

1. Pick the one story or technique that they revealed that most impressed you.

2. Write a simple statement that summarizes that story.

3. Write how you think you can use this lesson or technique in your work in the future.

IN
CONCLUSION

So, now we are at the end of our little journey through "the land of magic and make believe." Perhaps you have already experimented with writers, tried your hand with actors in casting, rehearsal, and production. And you've had the pleasure of reading the words of wisdom from some of my favorite wizards.

Now it is time for you to venture out on your own. Be bold, be courageous. That is how you will learn.

Stay in touch. If you have questions, or if you think you have unearthed or developed tricks of your own that you want to share, drop me a line at *mark@markwtravis.com*.

ABOUT
THE AUTHOR

Acclaimed as "the director's director," Mark W. Travis is regarded by many Hollywood and international professionals as one of the world's leading authorities on the art and craft of film directing. Drawing from his impressive background in design, writing, acting, and his wide range of experience directing theater, film, and television, Mark is able to bring new insights and exceptional clarity to the complex task of directing the feature film.

DIRECTING
Mark W. Travis earned a B.A. degree in Theatre at Antioch College and did his graduate training in Directing in the MFA program at the Yale School of Drama. Mark is a creative consultant to film directors Mark Rydell, George Tillman, Cyrus Nowrasteh, and many other notable writers and directors.

Mark's television directing credits include *The Facts of Life*, *Family Ties*, *Capitol*, and the Emmy Award-winning PBS dramatic special, *Blind Tom: The Thomas Bethune Story*. In 1998 he directed the pilot for *LifeStories*.

In 1990 he completed his first film, *Going Under*, for Warner Bros., starring Bill Pullman and Ned Beatty. In 2001 he wrote and directed *The Baritones* (parody of *The Sopranos*) as well as the short documentary, *Earlet*. In 2006 he co-directed the documentary, *Ancient Light*.

TEACHING

Mark's unique approach to working with actors and characters (The Travis Technique) has gained the attention of directors, writers and actors worldwide, and is becoming a standard approach for stimulating powerful performances.

Since 1992 Mark has been sharing his techniques on writing, acting and directing internationally. USA: The Directors Guild, American Film Institute, Pixar Animations Studios, UCLA Extension, Taos Talking Pictures Film Festival, Denver Film Festival, Hollywood Actor's Workshop, Hollywood Film Institute. JAPAN: Film & Media Lab and Vantan Film School. GERMANY: UW Filmseminares, ActionConcept, IFS, and HFF, the Munich Film School. POLAND: The Film Farm in Kotla. ENGLAND: Raindance, Paradigm Film Productions, Hurtwood House, Metropolitan Film School, National Film and Television School, London Film School, Lionhead Studios, London Film Academy. FRANCE: The Cannes Film Festival. NETHERLANDS: The Maurits Binger Institute. UKRAINE: Hollywood School in Ukraine. RUSSIA: International Film Actors Workshop. IRELAND: FAS Screen Training Ireland. NORWAY: The Norwegian Film School. DENMARK: The National Film School of Denmark. SPAIN: afilm International Film Workshops. CZECH REPUBLIC: FAMU Academy of Film and Television.

CONSULTING

Mark has served as a Creative Consultant on several feature films, including: *Here's Herbie, Notorious, Not Forgotten, The Stoning of Soraya M., Black Irish, Men of Honor, Barbershop, Barbershop 2, The Day Reagan Was Shot, Norma Jean, Jack and Me,* and television episodes of *Lois and Clark, The Pretender, Picket Fences, 90210, Melrose Place, Strong Medicine, NYPD Blue, The Practice,* and *Ally McBeal.*

WRITING

Mark is the author of the #1 best-seller (*L.A. Times*), *The Director's Journey: The Creative Collaboration Between Directors, Writers and Actors.* His second book on directing, *Directing Feature Films,* is currently used as required text in film schools worldwide.

Mark W. Travis
mark@markwtravis.com
markwtravis@gmail.com
www.markwtravis.com

Boyden Road Productions
10322 Mary Bell Avenue
Shadow Hills, CA 91040

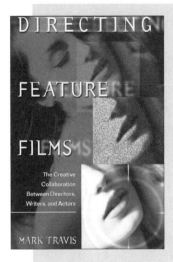

DIRECTING FEATURE FILMS
THE CREATIVE COLLABORATION BETWEEN DIRECTORS, WRITERS, AND ACTORS

MARK TRAVIS

The director is the guide, the inspiration, the focus that can shepherd hundreds of artists through the most chaotic, complex collaboration imaginable. But how does one person draw all these individuals together to realize a single vision?

Directing Feature Films takes you through the entire creative process of filmmaking – from concept to completion. You will learn how to really read a script, find its core, determine your vision, and effectively communicate with writers, actors, designers, cinematographers, editors, composers, and all the members of your creative team to ensure that vision reaches the screen.

This edition of the best-selling *The Director's Journey* contains new material on all aspects of filmmaking, taking the reader even deeper into the process.

"A comprehensive and inspired examination of craft. A must read for any serious professional."
    – Mark Rydell, Director, *On Golden Pond*, *James Dean*

"Mark Travis is the only practical teacher of directing I've ever met – and simply the best. I learned more from him than I did in four years of film school."
    – Cyrus Nowrasteh, Writer/Director
       The Day Reagan Was Shot

"With astonishing clarity Mark Travis articulates the techniques and skills of film directing."
    – John Badham, Director,
       Saturday Night Fever, *War Games*, *Blue Thunder*

MARK TRAVIS has directed motion pictures, television programs, and stage shows. A graduate of the Yale School of Drama, Mark has shared his techniques on directing in courses around the world. He has served as a directing consultant on many feature films and top-rated television series.

$26.95 · 402 PAGES · ORDER NUMBER 96RLS · ISBN: 9780941188432

FIRST TIME DIRECTOR
HOW TO MAKE YOUR BREAKTHROUGH MOVIE

GIL BETTMAN

FOREWORD BY ROBERT ZEMECKIS

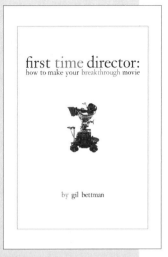

The first time director needs all the help he or she can get, especially on the set. That's what this book delivers. In the highly competitive marketplace where too many films vie for too little screen space, first time directors must meet the visual standards as established by Spielberg, Scorsese, and Stone. A tall order for any novice, but Gil Bettman arms you with the no-nonsense information and strategies to meet these ideals.

You'll learn:
· Walking the tightrope: How to maximize the director-producer relationship
· Going for the gold: Why "casting" is a job that never ends
· "Eye candy:" How to move your camera like Spielberg
· Silver bullets: Three quick fixes to make bad actors better and good actors great
· Lens craft: The under-appreciated art of picking lenses that heighten drama
· Teambuilding: How to make sure your key players on the set are all on the same page — and happy to be there
· Before and after: How to stay on top of the pre- and postproduction details that count the most

This book will enable you to pull form from chaos and make the best film possible — no matter your resources.

"Gil Bettman has lucidly set down the ABCs of directing so that dedicated students can learn exactly what will be required of them when they step onto a set."
> — from the Foreword by Robert Zemeckis, Director, *The Polar Express*; *Cast Away*; *What Lies Beneath*; *Contact*; *Forrest Gump*; *Back to the Future I, II, & III*; *Who Framed Roger Rabbit*; *Romancing the Stone*

"A valuable book by an experienced director that demystifies filmmaking."
> — Irvin Kershner, Director, *Star Wars: Episode 5 - The Empire Strikes Back*, *Never Say Never Again*, *Robocop 2*, *The Return of a Man Called Horse*

GIL BETTMAN has directed three feature films, dozens of primetime TV shows, and many top music videos. He is an Associate Professor in the School of Film and Television at Chapman University in Los Angeles.

$27.95 · 300 PAGES · ORDER NUMBER 113RLS · ISBN: 9780941188777

I'LL BE IN MY TRAILER!
THE CREATIVE WARS BETWEEN DIRECTORS & ACTORS

JOHN BADHAM & CRAIG MODDERNO

What do you do when actors won't do what you tell them to? Remembering his own awkwardness and terror as a beginning director working with actors who always had their own ideas, director John Badham (Saturday Night Fever, WarGames, Stakeout, The Shield) has a bookload of knowledge to pass along in this inspired and insightful must-read for directors at all levels of their craft.

Here are no-holds-barred out-of-school tales culled from celebrated top directors and actors like Sydney Pollack, Michael Mann, John Frankenheimer, Mel Gibson, James Woods, Anne Bancroft, Jenna Elfman, Roger Corman, and many more that reveal:

· The 10 worst things and the 10 best things you can say to an actor
· The nature of an actor's temperament and the true nature of his contributions
· The nature of creativity and its many pitfalls
· The processes of casting and rehearsal
· What happens in an actor's mind during a performance
· What directors do that alienates actors
· And much more

"Most young directors are afraid of actors. They come from film school with a heavy technical background, but they don't know how to deal with an actor. Even many experienced directors barely talk to their actors."
— Oliver Stone, Director, *JFK, Platoon, Wall Street, Born on the Fourth of July*

"Directors have needed a book like this since D.W. Griffith invented the close-up. We directors have to pass along to other directors our hard-learned lessons about actors. Maybe then they won't have to start from total ignorance like I did, like you did, like we all did."
— John Frankenheimer, Director, *The Manchurian Candidate, Grand Prix, Seconds*

JOHN BADHAM is the award-winning director of such classic films as *Saturday Night Fever, Stake Out*, and *WarGames* and such top TV shows as *Heroes, The Shield*, and *Crossing Jordan*. Badham currently is the DeMille Professor of Film and Media at Chapman University.

CRAIG MODDERNO is a contributing writer to the *New York Times*.

$26.95 · 243 PAGES · ORDER NUMBER 58RLS · ISBN: 9781932907148

MEMO FROM THE STORY DEPT.
SECRETS OF STRUCTURE AND CHARACTER

CHRISTOPHER VOGLER & DAVID MCKENNA

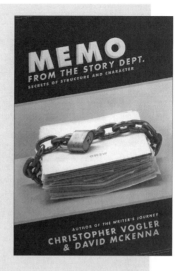

Memo From the Story Department is the long-awaited sequel to Christopher Vogler's immensely successful and influential handbook on mythic screenwriting, *The Writer's Journey: Mythic Structure for Storytellers and Screenwriters* (more than 250,000 copies sold). Vogler and his colleague, Columbia University film professor David McKenna, have produced an authoritative guide to advanced tools of structure and character development for screenwriters, novelists, game designers and film students. Users of the book will find a complete set of precision tools for taking their stories, step-by-step, through a quantum leap in writing quality.

"*Story structure is 90% of the game in screenwriting, though it's invisible on the page. Great movies have great structure — period. Nobody understands that better, and communicates it more brilliantly, than Mr. McKenna. His insight is a key reason I'm a working writer today.*"
— Mark Fergus, Oscar-nominated co-screenwriter, *Children of Men* and *Iron Man*

"*The way that Vogler and McKenna tag-team this book - it keeps you on your toes. Sometimes when you're yelling in the wilderness - it's good to have two voices. Certainly they'll give you perspectives on screenwriting that you've never seen before - and in this world of multiple screenwriting book choices - that's a good thing.*"
— Matthew Terry, filmmaker/screenwriter/teacher - columnist for
  www. hollywoodlitsales.com

Christopher Vogler is the top story analyst and consultant for major Hollywood studios and talent, advising on projects as varied as *The Lion King* and *Fight Club*. He wrote the script for the animated feature *Jester Till* and the story for a Japanese-style manga comic, *Ravenskull*. He was executive producer of the feature film *P.S. Your Cat is Dead* and has worked recently on projects for Will Smith, Helen Hunt, Roland Emmerich, and Darren Aronofsky. He travels widely to lecture about mythic structure. With Michael Hauge he produced the instructional DVD *The Hero's Two Journeys*. His book *The Writer's Journey* has been translated into ten languages and is one of the top-selling screenwriting manuals in the world.

David McKenna is a stage director, acting coach, voice-over artist and film professor at Columbia University and Barnard College. He is an expert on the films of Clint Eastwood and film genres including horror, westerns and war movies. His influential classes on screenwriting have stimulated a generation of young filmmakers and writers.

$26.95 · 280 PAGES · ORDER NUMBER 164RLS · ISBN 13: 9781932907971

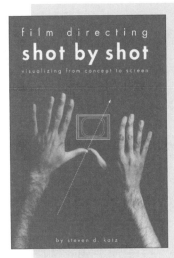

FILM DIRECTING: SHOT BY SHOT
VISUALIZING FROM CONCEPT TO SCREEN

STEVEN D. KATZ

BEST SELLER

Film Directing: Shot by Shot — with its famous blue cover — is the best-known book on directing and a favorite of professional directors as an on-set quick reference guide.

This international bestseller is a complete catalog of visual techniques and their stylistic implications, enabling working filmmakers to expand their knowledge.

Contains in-depth information on shot composition, staging sequences, visualization tools, framing and composition techniques, camera movement, blocking tracking shots, script analysis, and much more.

Includes over 750 storyboards and illustrations, with never-before-published storyboards from Steven Spielberg's *Empire of the Sun*, Orson Welles' *Citizen Kane*, and Alfred Hitchcock's *The Birds*.

"(To become a director) you have to teach yourself what makes movies good and what makes them bad. John Singleton has been my mentor... he's the one who told me what movies to watch and to read Shot by Shot.*"*
— Ice Cube, *New York Times*

"A generous number of photos and superb illustrations accompany each concept, many of the graphics being from Katz' own pen... Film Directing: Shot by Shot *is a feast for the eyes."*
— *Videomaker* Magazine

"... demonstrates the visual techniques of filmmaking by defining the process whereby the director converts storyboards into photographed scenes."
— *Back Stage Shoot*

"Contains an encyclopedic wealth of information."
— *Millimeter* Magazine

STEVEN D. KATZ is an award-winning filmmaker and also the author of *Film Directing: Cinematic Motion*.

$27.95 · 366 PAGES · ORDER NUMBER 7RLS · ISBN: 9780941188104

THE MYTH OF MWP

In a dark time, a light bringer came along, leading the curious and the frustrated to clarity and empowerment. It took the well-guarded secrets out of the hands of the few and made them available to all. It spread a spirit of openness and creative freedom, and built a storehouse of knowledge dedicated to the betterment of the arts.

The essence of the Michael Wiese Productions (MWP) is empowering people who have the burning desire to express themselves creatively. We help them realize their dreams by putting the tools in their hands. We demystify the sometimes secretive worlds of screenwriting, directing, acting, producing, film financing, and other media crafts.

By doing so, we hope to bring forth a realization of 'conscious media' which we define as being positively charged, emphasizing hope and affirming positive values like trust, cooperation, self-empowerment, freedom, and love. Grounded in the deep roots of myth, it aims to be healing both for those who make the art and those who encounter it. It hopes to be transformative for people, opening doors to new possibilities and pulling back veils to reveal hidden worlds.

MWP has built a storehouse of knowledge unequaled in the world, for no other publisher has so many titles on the media arts. Please visit www.mwp.com where you will find many free resources and a 25% discount on our books. Sign up and become part of the wider creative community!

Onward and upward,

Michael Wiese
Publisher/Filmmaker